COINS
THE BEGINNING COLLECTOR

COINS
THE BEGINNING COLLECTOR

ROBERT OAKES

ALL PHOTOGRAPHS © JAMES A. SIMEK

MALLARD PRESS

MALLARD PRESS
An imprint of
BDD Promotional Book Company, Inc.
666 Fifth Avenue
New York, New York 10103

A FRIEDMAN GROUP BOOK

Published by MALLARD PRESS
An imprint of BDD Promotional Book Company, Inc.
666 Fifth Avenue
New York, New York 10103

Mallard Press and its accompanying design and logo are trademarks of
BDD Promotional Book Company, Inc.

ISBN 0-792-45475-8

THE BEGINNING COLLECTOR: COINS
was prepared and produced by
Michael Friedman Publishing Group, Inc.
15 West 26th Street
New York, NY 10010

Photo Editor: Ede Rothaus

Additional photography: p.6/7; © John Gajda/FPG International

Typeset by Classic Type, Inc.
Color separations by Excel Graphic Arts Co.
Printed and bound in Hong Kong by Leefung-Asco Printers Ltd.

Dedicated to Mike Gumpel

CONTENTS

Introduction

Coin collecting may be the world's oldest hobby. Records indicate that the ancient Romans and the Greeks before them collected coins. (The Egyptians didn't collect coins because they hadn't perfected the art of minting coinage.) These ancients undoubtedly collected coins for a variety of reasons. Of course, one of the more important was to create a storehouse of wealth. But, judging by the coin hoards unearthed in recent years, the ancients also collected because they liked the beautiful images stamped on the coins. The Romans had coinage bearing likenesses of emperors such as Augustus or Nero. The Romans saved coins with portraits of popular people just as today we might save a poster of a famous person.

In addition to collecting coins because they were beautiful, the ancients had the desire to possess items of importance. Some Romans collected one of each new coin that was issued, apparently just to be able to show it off.

Coin collecting has remained popular through the years, and new collections are born in each new generation. Today, however, the field has a whole new dimension, one that the ancients and even those who collected just thirty or forty years ago never imagined. Today coin collecting has become big business. Each year Salomon Brothers, the Wall Street financial institution, rates the many different investment areas, among them stocks, bonds, real estate, gold—and rare coins.

Over the last fifteen years, coins have always ranked in the top ten in providing investment returns. For most of those years, they ranked number one, and in all but a very few years coins ranked in the top three. In other words, coins have consistently been, if not the very best, one of the best investments.

This fact has not been lost on collectors and investors. Today rare coins are sold not only by dealers in virtually every city in the country but also by top brokerage houses on Wall Street. You can buy limited partnerships and stock in companies that specialize in coin investing.

As a result there is a split in the field. On the one hand are the collectors who, while not adverse to making money on their collections, still buy coins primarily for their beauty and uniqueness, simply because they want to have them. On the other hand are numerous investors who know nothing about coins and really don't care; they see the field strictly as a way to make money.

What's interesting is that in today's world of coins, collectors are both the big winners and the big losers. Collectors are winners because they are the people who are most knowledgeable about coins. They understand rarity and quality and are in a position to obtain the best coins at the lowest prices. Today's coin collectors often grow wealthy off of their collections in just a few years.

But there is a down side, too. Collectors lose out because the price of collectible coins, especially the rarer ones, has grown so high that it is becoming increasingly expensive to start a collection.

In the old days (meaning twenty or thirty years ago), you could begin a coin collection simply by going through pocket change. Chances were that you would immediately find a coin or two worth more than its face value.

Today, however, all coinage is fiat, meaning that it's made out of non-precious base metals (such as copper, nickel, or zinc) rather than gold or silver. Furthermore, the coins are mass-produced in extremely large quantities, so unless there happens to be a minting error (such as a double strike, off-center strike, or other mistake), they are worth only their stated face value as a medium of exchange. They have no intrinsic, or metallic value.

As a result, to begin a collection you need to go to a dealer, club, or established collector who has surplus coins in order to buy them. Instead of searching through your change for needed dates, as in the good old days, modern coin collecting involves spending some money.

WHAT TO COLLECT?

It's often been said that the best way to invest in coins is to collect them as a hobby. As a collector you'll learn about coinage, and when you purchase a coin, you'll already know its background, its rarity, and its potential. You'll be in a position to put together not only a collection of great beauty but also of great value.

But, you have to begin somewhere. Where?

Generally speakings, there are several broad areas in which you can collect: United States, ancient, and coins from other countries are the most popular (although there are certainly collectors of medieval, renaissance, eastern coins, and so forth as well). Many people collect coins from their ancestral homeland. Coins from other countries, however, are difficult to build. In addition, they don't appreciate in value as much as homegrown coins. Hence, relatively few people collect coins from other countries.

Ancient coins have become incredibly popular. However, most are quite rare and their prices have quickly gone out of the reach of most beginners. (You can, of course, acquire a fine collection of ancient rare coins if you are willing to accept those in lesser condition. But most collectors really do want the better quality coins.)

In short, if you want to collect, there are plenty of coins out there waiting for you. In this book you'll learn how to get started and will come to understand the critical science of coin grading.

Coin collecting is a wonderful hobby and an excellent investment opportunity. You won't go wrong by devoting time and effort to it.

—Robert Oakes

THE HISTORY OF
COIN COLLECTING

Lydia (Asia Minor) electrum ¹/₃ stater. Struck between 650 and 561 BC, this coin, featuring a lion's head on the obverse and oblong punch on the reverse, is considered to be among the first coins minted in the world.

Lydian Electrum Coins (King Midas)	650–561 BC
Lydian Gold and Silver Coins (King Croesus)	560–546 BC

The first coins were struck by the kingdom of Lydia, a part of what is now Turkey, in Asia Minor. Tradition has it that the first king to issue gold coins was Midas.

According to legend, King Midas earned the favor of the god Dionysus, who granted him the power to have everything he touched turned to gold—the Midas touch—and he began minting gold coins. However, his "touch" soon turned out to be a curse because he couldn't eat without turning his food into gold. So Midas pleaded with Dionysus to remove the spell. Midas was told to bathe in the river Pactolus. He did and the Midas touch vanished.

Whether or not we give any credence to the legend that

Lydia (Asia Minor) light gold stater. Struck during the reign of King Croesus (561-546 BC), it shows both lion's and bull's heads on the obverse and an oblong punch on the reverse. This was the first use of refined gold in coinage.

Midas actually did strike the first coins, the fact is that the river Pactolus did provide the ancients of Lydia in the seventh century B.C. with electrum, a naturally-occurring alloy of gold and silver. The Lydian electrum coins, often bearing a lion's head, are thought by many to be the first coins ever minted.

At about the same time, the Greek empire was in its ascendency. Philip of Macedonia (Macedonia was in the area that is now modern Greece) conquered much of the northern Mediterranean. His son, Alexander, under the tutelage of the philosopher, Aristotle, conquered much of the rest of the known world. Along the way the coins of ancient Greece, primarily the tetradrachm, became the

Athens (Ancient Greece) silver tetradrachm (left). Struck between about 490 and 430 BC. The obverse has a portrait of the goddess Athena while the reverse shows one of her many symbols, the owl. This is probably one of the most famous of the ancient Greek coins. Roman (Republican) silver denarius (opposite). An anonymous issue struck between about 187 and 175 BC.

standard of commerce from Egypt and Syria to the coast of modern Portugal.

Throughout this period of history, the coins of ancient Greece reflected the greatness of the empire. The most famous were the "owl" coins of ancient Athens. On one side was a helmeted portrait of Athena, the goddess of wisdom. On the other was her symbol, the owl. The Athenians had access to silver mines at Laurium, and hence, the Greek coins were primarily silver.

The Greek empire was a loose coalition of city-states, most of which issued their own coins. As a result there were thousands of different minor Greek coins. Some of the most renowned were the Pegasus, or winged horse of Corinth, and the winged victory of Syracuse.

Hoards of coins have been discovered dating to the ancient Greeks that reveal that collectors of that period attempted to acquire silver coins from each of the city-states as well as the gold coins which were then being minted in Asia Minor.

THE ROMAN COINS AND COLLECTORS

Rome came to power in the third century B.C. and within a short half century dominated all of what had previously been the Greek empire. Unlike the Greeks, however, the Romans of the time were largely barbarians and did not have a well-developed civilization. This was evidenced by the fact that they did not, initially, have any precious metal (gold or silver) coinage. Roman coins were bronze, which did not wear well, and the coins were not well-received as instruments of trade. So, initially, the Romans borrowed and used silver Greek coins (in the same way they adopted many other aspects of the Greek civilization). Later, the Romans began minting their own silver coinage after the Greek model.

One of the first Roman silver coins was the didrachm, which featured a mythological figure on the obverse (front) and one of several animals on the reverse (back). It was soon replaced by the silver denarius. This coin was equal in value to ten *asses,* an *as* being a denomination of copper coin, much as a dime is equal in value to ten copper cents. The denarius quickly became the symbol of Rome and was recognized throughout the ancient world.

Coins in silver and gold featured the likenesses of the infamous as well as the emperors, such as Augustus, Claudius, Marcus Aurelius, Trajan, and Hadrian. Also depicted on the coins were some of the famous sea and land battles the Romans waged with their enemies over the course of hundreds of years.

Athenian   ca. 400 BC
Tetradrachm Coins
Era of the Greek
Collectors

Roman Republican
and Imperatorial
Coinage
Didrachm   ca. 250 BC
Silver Denarius   187–28 BC

Roman silver denarius of the Emperor Hadrian (left). Minted ca. AD 117-138. Roman silver denarius of Nero (under Claudius) (right). Struck ca. AD 51-54.

Ancient coin collectors (of which there were probably a great many) often would acquire all the issues of a particular favorite. For example, a collector might seek to acquire all the coins issued by the mad Nero. In fact, it was largely because of the ancient collectors that problems of counterfeit Roman coins were unearthed.

It turned out that enterprising individuals were minting their own versions of "official" coinage, except that these false coins were made with a copper or bronze center instead of pure silver. To help overcome this problem, in the first century A.D., the empire discouraged the minting of coins in all areas except Rome itself.

In Rome, sophisticated minting houses evolved that

cast aside the crude coin-making techniques of the earlier Romans. Professionals supervised the creation of the new coins. Using silver and gold from mines and recycled older coins, these moneyers created planchets, or round blanks. Then, expert die-makers created intricate designs for the coins. Finally, skilled strikers using heavy hammers imparted the designs onto the coins. As a result, the later Roman coinage was well-struck with marvelous artwork. Even today many examples of fine Roman coinage exist.

The Roman empire, however, began to decline from both inner dissension and constant warfare with savage tribes. As a result, the empire became poorer. Later emperors such as Caracalla debased (lowered the intrinsic value of)

A very rare Roman silver denarius (of the Imperatorial period) showing Cleopatra on one side and Marc Anthony on the other (left). Struck ca. 32 BC. Roman (Imperial) silver denarius of Augustus (right). Struck ca. AD 2-14.

Roman gold solidus of Honorius (left). Produced ca. AD 393-423. Byzantine gold solidus of the Emperor Justinian I (opposite). Struck at Constantinople ca. AD 550.

Roman Imperial
Coinage
Era of Roman
Collectors
Silver Denarius   27 BC–ca. AD 200
Gold Solidus   ca. AD 300

Byzantine Coins   ca. AD 200-1453

Coins of Justinian ca. AD 550
Era of Byzantine
Collectors

the coinage so that at that time (about A.D. 200), the denarius contained barely 40% silver. Later coins actually had only a thin layer, or veneer, of silver wash applied to a copper coin. Gold coins were made smaller and became quite scarce because they were hoarded for their metallic value.

In the fourth century A.D. Constantine I, the first Christian emperor, issued a new gold coin, the solidus, which became popular throughout the empire.

Hoards of Roman gold and silver coins that reveal that collectors of that era were sophisticated in their approach have been unearthed. Much as collectors of today, Roman collectors acquired coins of a particular emperor or of a particular period or all of the different types of coins issued. A real problem for collectors of the time, however, was that as each new issue of coinage came out, the minters would gather in the previous issues and melt them down to make the new coins. As a result, older coins became scarcer and some had significantly greater value.

BYZANTINE COINS

As the Roman empire declined, it was divided into two sections. The eastern Roman empire, whose capital was in Constantinople, survived the western Roman empire by nearly a thousand years. During that period it issued numerous coins modeled on the Roman coins. These became known as byzants or coins of Byzantium.

Certainly the most famous of the Byzantine emperors was Justinian. In the sixth century, his military victories were recorded in much of the gold and silver coinage. (Byzantium had less silver coinage than Rome.) Since Byzantium was largely a Christian empire, the coinage often shows crosses and Christian symbols.

Over the next half-millenium, the Byzantine empire shrank under repeated assaults by the Turks and by the tribes of Europe. Eventually only the city of Constantinople and a small area around it remained.

However, within that remarkable city was a dedicated group of collectors who acquired vast numbers of coins. Today, much of the coinage we have of ancient Byzantium is a result of the efforts of those early collectors.

Crusader Coins	1096–ca. 1300
Medieval Coins of France and Italy	ca. 1000–1460
Coins of the European Minters	1300–1700
Great European Collections (The Rothschilds)	1600–1900

MEDIEVAL COINAGE

During the last days of Byzantium in the east, western Europe began to flourish. A variety of small empires were born and died, and each issued coinage. During this period, these small states sent crusaders to capture Jerusalem, which had fallen into Arab hands after the decline of the western Roman empire.

Clockwise, from opposite, top, a Silver denier of the region of Achaia (located in the southernmost area of Greece, the Peloponnesos), minted in the late 1200s by Florent; from Mexico (colonial Spain), a 1793 silver eight reales (also known as the ''piece of eight''); from the American colonies, a Massachusetts pine tree shilling, one of the first types of coin to be struck in what is now the United States; Silver denier (variation of the word ''denarius'') of Aquitaine—Melle (France). Struck during the reign of Charles the Bald (AD 843-877).

Crusader coins as well as coins of France, Italy (particularly Venice), Spain, Portugal, the various states of Germany, and England began to emerge. The most popular of these, the gold ducat minted in Italy, became known worldwide.

At the same time, minting techniques improved. Even during the Renaissance a kind of mechanical revolution took place which allowed minters to come up with more perfectly round planchets to strike coins more accurately. As a result, the coinage of this period looks ''modern'' even by today's standards. A wide variety of coins that became known worldwide were struck. These included the famous English sovereigns, Spanish eight reales

(pieces of eight), and talers of Salzburg.

It was also during this period that the famous collections were started. The Rothschilds began collecting gold and silver coins that a century later would form the basis of one of Europe's most respected banks.

AMERICAN COINS

The first coins of the new world were actually of Spanish origin. They were produced by mints set up in cities of the Spanish colonies in Central and South America. Silver coins were struck in denominations of one, two, four, and eight reales (romantically called pieces of eight), while gold coins were made with values of one, two, four, and eight escudos (called doubloons).

The Spanish and Portuguese domination of South and Central America led to a wide variety of coins bearing the likenesses of the kings of those countries. However, by the nineteenth century, many of the former colonies were breaking away and magnificent new coinage featuring symbols of the indigenous people, such as the eagle and snake coins of Mexico, emerged.

In the early United States, coinage was a real problem. The only coins the early colonists had were those few they brought with them. Hence, shortages of coins were severe. In some cases, playing cards were pressed into service to be used as money!

Finally, Massachusetts set up its own mint under the direction of silversmith John Hull, who produced coins with oak, pine, and willow trees on them.

By the late seventeenth century, silver shillings were finding their way to America and the colonists had to get by with those and the Spanish reales.

It wasn't until after the Revolutionary War that real American coinage came into existence. Alexander Hamilton, the first Secretary of the Treasury, insisted Congress authorize United States coinage. It did, and in 1792 the first American coinage came out of Philadelphia.

Spanish Colonial Coins in the New World	1536–1857
U.S. Colonial Coins	1652–1790s
U.S. Coinage Authorized by Congress	1792
U.S. Coinage Commmences	1793

David Rittenhouse was named the first director and he quickly issued coins that became known the world over for their value and beauty. The first pieces authorized were:

$10.00	Gold Eagle
5.00	Gold Half Eagle
2.50	Gold Quarter Eagle
1.00	Silver Dollar
.50	Silver Half Dollar
.25	Silver Quarter Dollar
.10	Silver Disme (Dime)
.05	Silver Half Disme (Half Dime)
.01	Copper Cent
.005	Copper Half Cent

Of course, not all the coins were issued at once. The early mint initially had problems finding gold and silver bullion with which to make coins. Legend has it that George Washington contributed his silverware to make the first silver coins, the half dismes of 1792.

U.S. 1830 capped bust half dollar (opposite); (this page, left) U.S. 1795 capped bust, small eagle reverse, half eagle, or $5 gold. This is both the first year of issue for the denomination, and the first year that the gold coins were struck by the U.S. Mint; U.S. 1796 capped bust, small eagle reverse, eagle, or $10 gold.

Half Cent	1793–1857
Liberty Cap (Eckfeldt)	1793
Liberty Cap (Scot)	1794–1797
Draped Bust (Scot)	1800–1808
Classic Head (Reich)	1809–1836
Coronet (Gobrecht)	1840–1857

Perhaps the most famous early collector of coins in America was Benjamin Franklin. He encouraged others to save not only for the sake of having a hobby, but also in order to acquire wealth. Alexander Hamilton was also reputed to be a collector.

For years after the country was formed, America suffered from severe inflation. American gold and silver coins were frequently shipped abroad and melted for their metal content. Hence, shortages of coins were rampant.

During the days of the gold rush there were very few coins available to send out west. So, in the early 1850s, "territorial gold," or coins made by private mints, primarily in the west, were issued. Companies such as Moffat and Company and Augustus Humbert in San Francisco and F. D. Kohler, J. S. Ormsby, and others produced large quantities of gold coins which the miners used. Later most of these were exchanged for United States coinage and melted down by the government. Those that remain are considered treasures and bring very high prices from collectors.

The coin shortage became critical during the Civil War. The government issued paper money (green-backed dollars), which supposedly was backed by precious metal but which in reality was not. So, everyone sought out and hoarded gold and silver coins which had intrinsic metallic value. There simply was not enough coinage available to serve commerce.

To enhance commerce, particularly international trade, the Trade dollar was issued after the Civil War, in 1873. It had a slightly higher silver content and was intended to compete with dollar-sized coins issued by other countries.

By the beginning of the twentieth century, the government began issuing commemoratives. These were gold or silver coins which commemorated special events, people, and places. These included the Oregon Trail, the Pilgrim Tercentenary, the Panama-Pacific Exposition, and so on. Even today the government will occasionally issue a commemorative, such as the Statue of Liberty dollar.

U.S. 1986-S Statue of Liberty (Ellis Island) commemorative silver dollar. Proceeds from the sale of these coins went toward the restoration of the Statue of Liberty, as well as the facilities on Ellis Island, in commemoration of its 100th anniversary.

Also around the turn of the century some of the most beautiful American coins came into existence. The $20 double eagle (gold) coin created by Augustus Saint-Gaudens is considered by many to be the most perfectly designed coin ever minted by the United States.

During the Great Depression, Franklin Delano Roosevelt decreed that in order to avoid hoarding and deflation, the private ownership of gold was to be abolished. All minting of United States gold coins halted in 1933.

It was actually just before and during the Depression that great coin collections of this country were begun. Perhaps the most famous was that of the wealthy financier Bernard Baruch. Legend has it that in early 1929, Baruch stopped to have his shoes shined, and the shoeshine boy looked up and asked Baruch if he would like a stock tip. Baruch decided that if the market was so debased and popular that shoeshine boys had stock tips,

U.S. 1942-P Jefferson nickel. Because nickel was also considered a critical strategic metal during World War II, the mint from 1942 until 1945 struck five cent pieces in the alloy of copper, silver, and manganese. Therefore, calling this coin a nickel has only to do with tradition, since it contains no nickel at all.

the market must be overextended. He immediately sold all his stock and invested the funds in coins. When the crash came, he was secure and lived in wealth the remainder of his life.

Many other collectors of the 1930s and 1940s saw coins as a method of preserving wealth. Of course, there were those who simply collected for the pleasure of it. One of these was Abe Kosoff, a collector and later a dealer in coins who became one of the hobby's most respected leaders.

In the 1970s, Kosoff would sit at his booth at coin shows and sell coins he had acquired in the 1930s. He once remarked to a young boy who was purchasing a single large cent (the first United States cents were larger than today's cents) from him for $20 that he had bought an entire roll of the coins for $10 thirty years earlier!

CLAD COINS

During this century coinage has undergone numerous changes. Nothing has been more dramatic, however, than the switch from precious to base metals. In 1964 the United States was facing a serious coin shortage. Because of the rising price of the metal itself, partly due to inflation, the silver in United States coins was worth more than the face value of coins themselves. Therefore, collectors and investors were taking the coins out of circulation, melting them down, and selling the silver.

To solve the problem, the government, in 1965, began issuing clad (copper-nickel layers bonded to a core of pure copper) dimes and quarters, and reduced the net silver content of the half dollar from 90% pure to 40%, also using a similar cladding technique. In 1971 the half dollar, as well as the newly-issued Eisenhower dollar, became a casualty of ever-increasing metals prices, and all silver was removed from that denomination as well. Today, all dimes, quarters, and half dollars are made from the familiar "sandwich" composition, and even the venerable bronze cent is now made from copper-plated zinc. It seems as though we learned our monetary lessons well from the ancient Romans.

(Today, of course, the government also issues "eagles" in gold and silver, but these are not true circulating coins. Rather, their value is based on their content of the precious metal.)

MODERN MINTING

Just as coinage has changed, so too have mints and minting techniques. During the course of its history, the United States has had official mints in eight different locations. Each mint adds to the coin a tiny stamp, which indicates where the piece was minted. Since the same coins may be minted at several locations, collectors often seek to acquire a sample of coin from each mint.

Over the years the mints and their mint marks include:

MINT	MINT MARK
Charlotte, North Carolina (1838–1861)	C
Carson City, Nevada (1879–1893)	CC
Dahlonega, Georgia (1838–1861)	D
Denver, Colorado (1906–present)	D Current
New Orleans, Louisiana (1838–1909)	O
Philadelphia, Pennsylvania (1793–present)	P Current
San Francisco, California (1874–present)	S Current
West Point, New York (1984–present)	W Current

NOTE: Coins struck at the Philadelphia mint prior to 1979 do not have a mint mark (except for five-cent coins made during the World War II period of 1942–1945). Cents struck at Philadelphia still do not have a mint mark.

Modern minting involves the use of huge hydraulic presses. Engravers create dies out of polished hardened steel. These dies are then inserted into the machine and blank planchets, previously stamped out of sheets of metal, are fed through at an incredible rate of speed. Dies simultaneously strike the obverse (front) and reverse (back)

Copper-nickel clad coinage was introduced in 1965 for U.S. dimes and quarter dollars, and in 1971 for half dollars and "Ike" dollars, and in 1979 for the Susan B. Anthony dollars. From 1965 through 1970, half dollars (above) were struck in a silver-clad composition, the resulting coins containing a net amount of 40 percent pure silver. Some collector edition (non-circulating) "Ike" dollars from 1971 through 1974, as well as some collector bicentennial quarters, half dollars, and dollars of 1976, were also made in the same manner, as were some later commemorative issues.

of the coins. Millions of coins are produced daily in this fashion.

Because the dies are handmade for all the mints in Philadelphia and hand-positioned in the presses, however, occasional errors occur. Sometimes dates from different years will be superimposed. Occasionally there will be double strikes or other errors. These error coins are highly prized by collectors. (See the last chapter, "Error Coins, Fakes and Counterfeits," for more details.)

COLLECTORS TODAY

Today's collectors tend to specialize in coins issued, generally speaking, before the 1930s. The simple reason is that these tend to be the rarer pieces. Coins issued during the 1940s and later, are still so plentiful as to not warrant serious collecting. (Although recent price appreciation for some of the earlier dates of these has caught collectors' eyes.)

U.S. 1926-D standing Liberty quarter dollar. One can buy circulated examples of the later dates of this coin for just a few dollars each.

How to Get Started

U.S. 1871 two cent piece. Minted from 1864 until 1873. Heightened religious sentiment apparent during the Civil War caused this coin to be the first to carry the motto, ''In God We Trust.''

Which coins you collect is often determined more by your pocketbook than anything else. However, many collectors do show marked preferences. For example, a person with strong religious beliefs might collect coins with Biblical themes. A person who is a doctor might collect any coins that have to do with medicine. History buffs might collect Civil War coins or coins of ancient Rome and Greece.

Investors, on the other hand, don't really care what kinds of coins they purchase, as long as the coins appreciate in value quickly. As noted in earlier chapters, these are usually United States coins that are more than fifty years

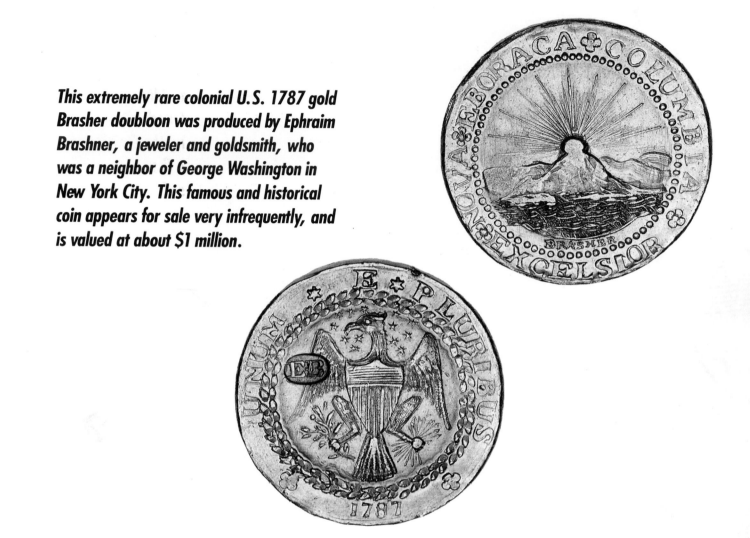

This extremely rare colonial U.S. 1787 gold Brasher doubloon was produced by Ephraim Brashner, a jeweler and goldsmith, who was a neighbor of George Washington in New York City. This famous and historical coin appears for sale very infrequently, and is valued at about $1 million.

old, and ancient coins (for collectors with deep pockets).

Regardless of which coins you decide to collect, you will need to know what determines a coin's value. Why is one coin worth a thousand dollars to a collector and another, similar-looking coin, worth only fifty cents?

RARITY

Although it may seem obvious, many people overlook this factor in determining a coin's value. The fewer examples of a particular coin that there are, the more valuable that coin is. For example, one of the most well-known American coins is the legendary 1804 silver dollar. Only

Two Cents (Longacre)	1864–1873
Three Cents—Silver (Longacre)	1851–1873
Three Cents—Nickel (Longacre)	1865–1889

U.S. 1800 draped bust type, large, or heraldic, eagle reverse silver dollar.

eight originals and seven restrikes are known to exist. When one of these comes onto the market, the price for it is phenomenal, always well into six figures.

On the other hand, you can pick another silver dollar of roughly the same period, such as the 1801 silver dollar, of which 54,454 were struck, and the price is only 1/100th the price of the 1804 coin. What's the difference? Rarity. The rarer the coin, the greater its value.

Judging rarity, however, is a very tricky business. The quantity minted for all U.S. coins is readily known from official mint records, although in its early years, the mint would commonly use dies (which were very expensive to make) until they literally wore out, regardless of the date

U.S. 1804 silver dollar. Perhaps the most famous coin in the United States series, it is known as the king of the American coins. Only fifteen pieces were minted (interestingly between 1834 and 1860), and the information written about this one coin over the past 150 years would fill volumes. This date is valued at over $1 million.

stamped on them. In the example above, although mint records indicate that 19,570 silver dollars were made in 1804, numismatic scholars have conclusively proven that they were most likely dated 1803, and that the fifteen 1804 dollars were struck in later years.

Although mintage figures are useful as a relative guide, what is not known is how many of the coins were lost or melted down over the course of time. A coin may have started out with 100,000 being minted. But during its life span of a hundred years, 99,000 of the pieces may have been destroyed. Thus, what was once common, may now be rare—no one knows for sure. This is the challenge of collecting.

U.S. 1850 coronet type large cent.

QUALITY

The second most important (some say it's the first) consideration when purchasing a coin is its quality, a fragile commodity. An old "Hawaii Five-O" television show centered on a supposedly rare nickel. When the hero was being chased by crooks and wanted to hide the coin, he deposited it in a newspaper stand. The audience was supposed to believe that it would be safe there until it could be retrieved later on.

Of course, collectors watching the show cringed. Dropping a truly valuable coin into a batch of other coins would most certainly harm it, and its value would be diminished.

U.S. 1865 Liberty seated silver dollar.

The reason, quite simply, is that coins are most treasured only when they are in pristine condition. In other words, the closer to mint state that they are, the more valuable. Any nicks, scratches, abrasions, or even fingerprints, detract from a coin's value.

Some coins are even better. These are proofs, or coins that are struck several times on specially selected blanks, or planchets, at the mint and have a highly polished reflective surface. They are designed to be sold strictly to collectors. Proofs sometimes command very high prices, depending on their rarity.

In most cases, however, preservation is the key to a coin's value. If, during the fifty or hundred years the coin

Large Cent	1793–1857
Chain (Voigt)	1793
Flowing Hair (Eckfeldt)	1793
Liberty Cap (Wright, Gardner)	1793–1796
Draped Bust (Scot)	1796–1807
Classic Head (Reich)	1808–1814
Coronet (Scot, Gobrecht)	1816–1857

has been in existence, it gets even a single scratch or fingerprint, its value could drop by half! We'll say a lot more about grading coins in subsequent chapters.

HOW TO HOLD A RARE COIN

Let's just take a moment to consider how a collector *holds* a coin. Today, most top-grade coins come sealed in plastic, so you can hold them any way you want. However, when you're just beginning to collect, you may be buying less than top-grade coins, and they might not be protected.

When someone offers you a coin to look at, perhaps with a hope that you'll buy it, never, never pick up the coin and lay it in your hands or allow your fingers to touch either the obverse or reverse sides. The natural moisture and chemicals in your skin will damage its surface.

Instead, pick it up carefully by the rim. Hold it between your thumb and middle finger gingerly and look at both sides. It's a good idea to hold it over a piece of felt so that if you drop it, it won't roll off the counter and fall to the floor.

If you really want to see the surface, use a magnifier. Between five and ten power is best. Anything stronger will distort the image and make viewing more difficult.

One last thing. Don't breathe on the coin. The moisture from your breath can also damage the surface.

BUILDING YOUR COLLECTION

The old rule in coin collecting, which still holds today, is to buy the best quality coins you can afford. The reason, simply, is that when coin values go up, the better the quality, the faster the appreciation. In a hot coin investment market, a middle-of-the-road coin may only double in value. But the price of the same coin in top condition

U.S. 1877 trade dollar. Slightly heavier in weight (therefore containing more silver) than the circulating silver dollar, it was authorized expressly to compete in foreign trade and commerce (particularly in the Orient) with dollar-sized coins of the other countries.

could go up by a factor of ten (it's happened more than once in the past).

When you get started, you may simply buy lesser quality coins because you can't afford the top grades. But, as soon as your pocketbook allows, upgrade your collection. Sell your lesser-grade coins and buy better grades. Wise collectors continually upgrade their collections.

WHERE TO FIND COINS

As noted earlier, in the old days you could begin a collection simply by searching your pocket change. Years ago a young collector could go to small grocery stores at the end

Small Cent	1856–date
Flying Eagle (Longacre)	1856–1858
Indian Head (Longacre)	1859–1909
Lincoln (Brenner)	1909–1958
Wartime steel (Brenner)	1943
Memorial rev. (Gasparro)	1959–date

of the day and help count their change, and then buy the coins for paper currency. Then the child could take the change home and carefully examine the coins. Not a day would go by when a Mercury dime, rare Lincoln cent, or some other coin that was worth more than its face value would pop up.

Since the introduction of clad coinage, however, this type of collecting is no longer really possible. Today, searching pocket change is likely to turn up just a bunch of worn clad coins. The best you can hope for is to find an occasional error piece.

Instead, in order to find rare coins today, you have to buy them. There are four major sources: rare-coin dealers; rare-coin clubs; rare-coin shows; and rare-coin auctions.

BUYING FROM DEALERS

Until you become quite knowledgeable in rare coins, a coin dealer is probably your best source for coins and information. Until you learn, you will have the dealer's expertise to fall back on.

Many dealers cater to new collectors by putting up "bid boards." These are literally boards onto which are pinned, taped, or clipped rare coins (in holders, of course). You get to look at the coins and then write the amount you want to pay onto a bid sheet for the coin. When the auction ends, the coin goes to the highest bidder.

Bid boards can be a wonderful and exciting way to get into rare-coin collecting. They allow you to meet other collectors, to exchange information and to gain knowledge. (Just be sure the dealer is honest and that the bid board contains coins from other collectors, not junk the dealer wants to get rid of.)

Of course, you can go to the dealer directly. One way to start is to bend a dealer's ear. Ask questions. Be aware,

Venice (Italy) silver ducato. Issue of Giovanni Corner II (1709-1722).

however, that successful dealers won't have a lot of time for a new collector. Coins today are big business, and dealers are frequently on the phone making deals.

If, however, you want a specific coin, you can find it at a dealer. If the dealer doesn't have it, you can ask him or her to get it for you. Many beginning collectors will put out a "want list." This is simply a listing of coins that they want and the prices they are willing to pay. Assuming the dealer isn't into high finance (many are) and that the price you're willing to pay is reasonable, the dealer will try to secure a coin for you.

There is one last, great advantage of buying from a dealer. If, over the years, you establish a rapport with a

Five Cents	1866–date
Shield (Longacre)	1866–1883
Liberty Head (Barber)	1883–1913
Indian/Buffalo (Fraser)	1913–1938
Jefferson (Schlag)	1938–date
Wartime silver (Schlag)	1942–1945

dealer, that relationship will always be there for you. Not only will the dealer be keeping an eye open for coins that you want, but when you want to sell, the dealer will buy your coins back from you.

PROBLEMS WITH BUYING FROM DEALERS

On the other hand, there can be problems with buying coins from dealers. If the dealer is unscrupulous, and a few are, he may charge you too much for a coin. If you're just starting out, you may not know the difference.

For example, the dealer may show you a coin that he says is graded MS-63 (we'll get into coin grades in the next chapter). The dealer brings out the *Greysheet,* a weekly publication that lists current coin prices and shows you that the retail price for the coin is $200. You buy it.

However, a week later you decide to sell. You bring it back to the dealer, who looks at it through a magnifier and says "Nope that's only an MS-60. It's only worth $35. I'll buy it back from you at wholesale, twenty bucks!"

This is much less of a problem with higher grade investment coins, which carry grading certificates, but can be a real problem with new collectors who often buy less expensive, lower grade coins.

The best way to avoid such problems is to start out small with a dealer. Buy a few inexpensive coins from him. Then attempt to resell them to him. You'll learn very quickly just how honorable he really is.

Note: You will never be able to immediately sell your coin for what you paid for it. Dealers must make a profit to stay in business. Typically their margin is 20 percent. If you buy a coin for $20, you will be able to resell it immediately for only about $16. You'll have to wait until it goes up in value before you'll be able to sell it for what you paid—or maybe even sell it for more.

A $20 private issue of Kellogg & Co., San Francisco, California. Vast quantities of private and semi-official gold pieces were struck by numerous individuals following the gold rush, but the establishment of a U.S. Mint in San Francisco in 1854 virtually put a halt to the private issues in that part of the country.

MAIL-ORDER DEALERS

Many dealers will sell—and buy—coins through the mail. Typically their offers to sell are not firm. They are based on the price of the coin at the time they placed an ad. It may be weeks or months later when you see their ad. Therefore, always call first to inquire as to the condition of the coin the dealer is selling and the current price.

Mail-order dealers usually will offer you a full refund for a short period of time, typically five days. You send them payment and they'll send you the coin. If you don't think the coin is all they said it would be, you send it back, and your money is returned.

At least that's the way it's supposed to work. A good

Half Dime	1794–1873
Flowing Hair (Scot)	1794–1795
Draped Bust/ Sm. Eagle (Scot)	1796–1797
Draped Bust/ Lg. Eagle (Scot)	1800–1805
Capped Bust (Kneass)	1829–1837
Liberty Seated (Gobrecht)	1837–1873

piece of advice is to do the same thing with a mail-order dealer as you would with an over-the-counter dealer. Start off small and see how the dealer operates. Try returning a coin. If there are no problems, then you're probably safe to plow along with building a collection. If there are problems, it is probably best to shop elsewhere. While complaining to the postal authorities rarely brings satisfaction, because of their workload, by all means make the publication where the advertisement appeared aware of the situation. You will generally find them eager to help since, for obvious reasons, they want to rid their publications of advertisers who have chronic complaints made against them. All major publications conduct random tests of their advertisers in a continuing effort to alleviate this problem.

CHOOSING A DEALER

Whether it's over-the-counter or mail-order, here are some tips for picking a good dealer:

1. Be sure the dealer has a professional affiliation. Look for PNG (Professional Numismatists Guild—a coalition of dealers); ANA (American Numismatic Association—every collector can and should belong); and ANS (American Numismatic Society—for more elite collectors).

2. Ask how long the dealer has been in business. The longer the better.

3. Go to a dealer who belongs to a network. Today dealers are linked by satellite coin networks. They buy and sell coins wholesale over this network. Belonging to one indicates, if nothing else, that the dealer is quite active in the business.

4. Make sure the dealer can deliver. A reputable dealer will let you know right away if he or she has the coin and will sell it to you. If the dealer doesn't have it on hand, he or she will try to get it for you. A disreputable dealer will tell you the coin is in stock, when it isn't, and try to stall

U.S. 1913 Indian head eagle, or $10 gold. This design by Augustus St. Gaudens.

you while attempting to locate it. In the worst case, the dealer will ask for your money up front and then let you wait weeks while attempting to track down the coin you want. Although good advice is never to pay for a coin until you get it, exceptions could include ordering from a reputable mail-order dealer, or having a reputable retail dealer ask you for a reasonable deposit for a coin you specifically ask him to acquire for you. This is a fair request, and is done to protect the dealer's financial interest.

5. Does the dealer have time to talk to you? Some dealers are into high finance. The coin market today does many millions of dollars of business every year. If the dealer is too big for you, he or she won't have time to

U.S. 1976-D Eisenhower dollar with bicentennial reverse (left); U.S. 1976-D half dollar with bicentennial reverse (right); U.S. 1976 quarter dollar with bicentennial reverse.

help you get started. You're better off finding a dealer who has a smaller business and more time to spend on your collection.

BUYING FROM COIN CLUBS

Coin clubs are like computer users' groups. They are places where people of similar interests can get together to share and learn.

Becoming involved with a coin club in your area (check with dealers to find out if there is one) is an excellent way to get started collecting. Frequently there are established

collectors who are more than willing to take you aside and help. They'll teach you the basics and give you advice that will aid you your entire collecting life.

In addition, coin clubs frequently have small shows where members can trade, buy, and sell coins. Typically these are inexpensive coins and, consequently, it's another excellent way for the beginner to get started.

BUYING AT COIN SHOWS

Coin shows are held all over the country. There's a show somewhere every weekend. Chances are that if you live in a metropolitan area, one takes place near you several times a year. To find out about coin shows, check with dealers or with coin publications. *Coin World* is a weekly that lists the shows around the country.

At a coin show, the dealers set up booths to display the coins they have for sale. There may be hundreds of dealers there, and the show may take up an entire convention center. Most beginners, however, are disappointed at coin shows. The reason is that in recent years these have turned into wholesale shows. Although the coin-collecting public is welcome, typically the real business takes place between the dealers. They buy and sell between themselves and fill their clients' want lists. Many dealers at shows simply won't have time to talk to you and some can be rude about saying so. If you have thin skin, stay away from coin shows.

On the other hand, probably the majority of dealers are more than willing to show you their coins and take time to help you, if they believe you really will buy and aren't just looking and wasting their time. Plan to spend an afternoon or an entire day at a coin show. It'll take that long just to get around to all the booths.

COIN AUCTIONS

Some say the best way to buy rare coins is at an auction. Presumably, you get the best prices at auctions. Sometimes this is true… sometimes it isn't.

Auction houses offer the rarest coins for sale to the public. Bids may be made in person or, depending on the sale, through the mail. Typically, both the buyer and the seller pay a 10% commission to the auction house. The coins are usually made available for inspection several weeks before the actual auction takes place.

BEAUTY IS IN THE EYE OF THE BEHOLDER

Finally, there is the matter of the appearance of the coin itself. Some coins, such as the Susan B. Anthony dollar, are judged by the public to be ugly coins. Others, such as the Mercury dime or the Buffalo nickel, are considered beautiful.

While the beauty of a coin is really just a personal preference, it often helps to determine value. More beautiful coins are more desired and the demand for them is larger. Ugly coins are less desired and less in demand. Since demand contributes to value, the more beautiful the coin, generally speaking, the more valuable it will be.

When getting started, probably the best advice is to pick a series of coins that look beautiful to you. One man chose to collect Hawaiian coins because he loved the way they looked. He amassed a large collection for next to nothing because little was known about these coins and few people collected them. But, eventually they became popular and when they did, the value of his collection jumped tenfold.

1883 Hawaiian quarter dollar, issue of King Kalakaua I. The 1883 silver coinage of the Kingdom of Hawaii has many ties to the U.S. The designs were prepared by Charles Barber, chief engraver of the U.S. Mint at Philadelphia where the dies were manufactured. Their weight, fineness, and size standards were equal to their U.S. counterparts, and they were struck at the U.S. Mint in San Francisco. And by presidential order, they were redeemable at par with U.S. coins until 1904. They are interesting and historical reminders of a time when our current fiftieth state was a kingdom of its own.

Auction houses regularly advertise in publications such as *Coin World*, noted above, or *COINage*, the largest-circulation coin magazine published monthly.

Usually, unless you are a very experienced and knowledgeable collector, you'd best not attempt to buy coins at auction. The rule at auctions is *caveat emptor* which in Latin means "Let the buyer beware." The fact that a coin is in a holder marking it as top quality does not mean that it truly is valuable. Unless you know what you're buying, you can easily be cheated at an auction, and could end up spending a great deal of money for something worth a lot less than you thought.

On the other hand, one man recently bought a box of coins at auction. The lot included a group of proof coins and mint sets. (Proof coins and mint sets are coins made by the mint for sale to collectors.) When he got the box

Dime	1796–date
Draped Bust/ Sm. Eagle (Scot)	1796–1797
Draped Bust/ Lg. Eagle (Scot)	1798–1807
Capped Bust (Reich, Kneass)	1809–1837
Liberty Seated (Gobrecht)	1837–1891
Liberty Head (Barber)	1892–1916
"Mercury" (Weinman)	1916–1945
Roosevelt (Silver) (Sinnock)	1946–1964
Roosevelt (Clad) (Sinnock)	1965–date

home and began taking out the coins, he found that at the bottom there were about a dozen rare gold coins that the auctioneers apparently were not aware of. The gold coins were worth more than $10,000, ten times what he had paid for the box!

The allure of finding hidden treasure remains one of the biggest inducements to buying at auction.

HOW TO NEGOTIATE BUYS

A final and an excellent method of buying at auction (or elsewhere) is to negotiate with a dealer with whom you've established a relationship. A typical arrangement is to have the dealer go to the auction (presumably it's one he's already planning to attend) and buy a predetermined number of coins for you in a given condition and for below a set price. For his services you will compensate the dealer by paying him 5 or 10 percent over the cost of coins. If you have a good dealer who is honest, you should end up with good coins.

SELLING COINS

Selling your collection is like buying, only in reverse. You use the same sources—an over-the-counter dealer, a mail-order dealer, a club, or an auction. Just keep in mind that in order to sell to these people, you'll have to accept about 20 percent below retail—that's their profit margin.

You can, of course, sell directly. There's nothing to prevent you from taking out an ad in one of the publications mentioned above and selling your coins directly to another collector. It may take longer, but it could be worth the wait. And along the way you could learn a great deal about the field.

BARTER

Ultimately, getting started with a coin collection

French gold Louis d'Or, 1786. Issue of Louis XVI.

involves bartering. Although the medium of exchange is money, what you end up doing is acquiring rare coins and then bartering them for coins of better quality until you have a truly magnificent collection.

As long as you remember that the word *barter* is derived from the French word, *bareter*, which actually means "to cheat," you'll be okay. In the coin field, while parties don't usually try to cheat one another, they do try to make money on each trade or deal. That's the challenge.

Once you get involved and begin to make a few good trades, you'll find that collecting gets into your blood. You won't want to stop.

Caring For Your Coins

Turolian (Austrian) silver taler minted during the reign of Archduke Ferdinand (1564-1595).

Coins are simply pieces of metal—usually copper, silver, nickel, or gold. With the exception of gold, all of these metals tend to oxidize. And all of them are subject to scratches and abrasions.

Since a coin's value is determined to a great degree by its condition, it behooves every collector to take the utmost precaution to see that a coin isn't damaged during storage. A properly protected coin will not diminish due to wear. Here are some keys to protecting your collection:

Individual Storage—A rare coin should always be stored in an individual container. Never put two or more coins together. No matter how carefully you separate them in a single container, the opportunity for them to

U.S. 1879 Liberty head, or Morgan type, silver dollar.

bang together always exists. Each time one coin touches another you increase the risk of damaging the coins with scratches and dents.

Storage Containers—Be very careful of the type of container that you use. In the past, many copper cents were stored in paper containers made especially for coins. Unfortunately, the paper contained a sulphur compound that reacted with the copper to stain and pit the coins. While tarnish, or "toning," on silver coins is sometimes considered attractive, it is almost never considered to be an asset to copper coins. And pitting severely affects the coins' value.

Today special *non-reactive* plastic containers are availa-

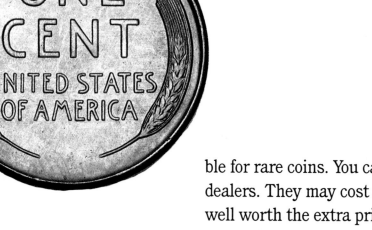

U.S. 1943-D Lincoln head cent. As copper was needed for the wartime effort (mostly to make bullet shell casings), the U.S. Mint, in 1943, made cents from zinc-plated steel.

ble for rare coins. You can obtain these from most coin dealers. They may cost a small amount more, but they are well worth the extra price. As an alternative, if you have your coin "slabbed", be sure that the grading service guarantees that the plastic container that encases your coin won't hurt the coin.

Storage Security—Once you have your coins safely placed in non-reactive individual containers, you should consider long-term storage. Most collectors keep their coins in bank safety deposit boxes. These deposit boxes do have the drawback of limited accessibility. But this is usually outweighed by their security.

If you do keep your coins at home, don't advertise the fact that you're a coin collector. Unfortunately, robberies of valued collections are all too common.

ORGANIZING YOUR COINS

Once you acquire more than a dozen coins, organizing them can become a problem. Most beginning collectors use the file card method. Each time you acquire a coin you fill out on a separate card:

Grade

Cost to you

Date you acquired it

Intention (do you plan to sell or hold?)

Other pertinent information

In this way you can keep track of your entire collection on paper while it remains safely secured in a bank vault.

As you expand your collection, you may want to keep track of it on your home computer. There are many programs available today designed especially for coin collectors. Here are a few, and their most appropriate use. (The following material is reprinted with permission from *COINage Magazine*.)

COINS/PLUS from Compu-Quote

IBM and compatibles, 5¼" or 3½" formats, 384K RAM minimum, MS-DOS 2.1 or higher, hard disk recommended. Apple II, 3½" or two 5¼" drives, ProDOS, 128K RAM (for the Apple IIe, must have 65C02 CPU chip) Macintosh, 512 K RAM, 800K floppy or hard disk.
Who should use this program:

Collector/Investor

Those who want to have their coin values
automatically updated

Those who are unfamiliar with computers

Who should not use this program:

Larger dealers

The documentation is quite good and the program is menu driven. Even a first-time user should have no problems here.

COINS/PLUS from CompuQuote, 6914 Berquist Ave., Canoga Park, CA 91307

COIN ELITE from Trove Software

IBM and compatibles, 5¼" or 3½" formats, 256K RAM minimum, MS-DOS 2.0 or higher

Coin Elite is a program which allows you to quickly and easily create an inventory of your coins, their condition and their value.

Who should use this program:

> Collectors/Dealers with a large inventory of coins
> Those unfamiliar with computers (menu driven)
> When specific reports are required (you can design your own reports)

Who should not use this program:

> Collectors with small portfolios

Coin Elite, from Trove Software, P.O. Box 218, Olathe, KS 66061

COMPUTERIZED COLLECTIBLES from Dynamic Software

IBM and compatibles, 5¼" formats, 256K RAM minimum, MS-DOS 2.0 or higher and a minimum 5 MB hard disk

Available in full-size for dealers and reduced size for investors.

Perhaps the most intriguing feature of the program is its ability to generate mailing labels and 2 × 2 coin description flips (for use with plastic coin containers). The flips allow you to enter a variety of information including price, grade and coin description.

Who should use this program:

> Dealers and collectors with very large portfolios who are constantly trading
> Those with an understanding of data/base programs

Who should not use this program:

> Collectors and investors with small to medium sized portfolios
> Those who are unfamiliar with computers
> Those who want automatic updating

From Dynamic Software, Inc., 4942 Highpoint Dr., Marietta, GA 30066

NUMISMATIC DATA MANAGER *from Double Eagle Development*

IBM and compatibles, 5¼" or 3½" formats, 512K RAM minimum, MS-DOS 2.0 or higher, hard disk

Numismatic Data Manager provides sophisticated tracking of your coin portfolio. It's menu driven system is easy to understand and it has the capacity to handle a large number of coins.

Who should use this program:

> Investors and collectors
>
> Small Dealers

Who should not use this program:

> Large dealers
>
> Those who want automatic updating

Numismatic Data Manager from Double Eagle Development, 1271 W. Dundee Rd., Suite 13A, Buffalo Grove, IL 60089

COINCOLLECTOR *from NumiSoft*

IBM PC, XT, AT-286 or 386 clone or compatible MS-DOS version 3.2 or better, 256K RAM memory (more preferable would be 384 or 512), 20-Megabyte ROM storage (recommended for an application's extensive data storage requirements. Although it would be possible to run an application on a floppy-drive only machine, it would be very time-consuming and difficult)

Who should use this program:

> Collectors and investors who also have an extensive background in computers and programming in the IBM environment and specifically the COBOL language.

Who should not use this program:

> Collectors and investors who are in any way new to computers.

It's not hard if you know computers. If you don't you could be lost before you start.

Coincollector, from NumiSoft, P.O. Box 933, Auburn, WA 98071

How Coins Are Graded

A coin's value is largely determined by its quality, as discussed in the last chapter. The closer to mint condition, the more valuable the coin. The more wear and tear, the less valuable. But how do we determine the condition of a particular coin? What one person views as very good condition, another may see as very poor. Whose opinion counts?

This question has bothered hobbyists since coin collecting began. As a result, today we have high-grade coins encased in plastic bearing a certificate stating their condition. Unfortunately, many of these certificates themselves have come into question.

To understand how coins are graded and the value of

certificates and plastic-encased coins, we must really see how the hobby has progressed to where it is today. That's what we'll discuss in this chapter.

DESCRIPTIVE GRADING

After the turn of the century, but particularly after the 1920s, collectors and dealers used a descriptive system to grade coins. Roughly speaking, here's what the system looks like:

PROOF A special coin struck by the mint just for collectors. This technically is not a grade.

UNCIRCULATED This describes a coin that was intended for circulation but for one reason or another never reached the public. It is brand new and pristine. (A coin close to this grade, but with some minor wear might be called *about uncirculated*.)

FINE This coin reached circulation, and shows some wear and tear. A grade above this would be *extremely fine* and would mean there was almost no visible wear, with some of the original mint luster showing. A grade below would be *about fine* and there would be considerable wear.

GOOD The coin is almost worn out. The design, however, must be visible and the lettering readable.

THE NEW INVESTORS

As long as the hobby was limited to collectors and a few dealers, many of whom knew each other, this system worked. For example, Pete knew that Harry tended to grade a bit high, and compensated for it. Harry knew that Pete graded low and likewise compensated.

By the 1970s, however, this system began to prove inadequate. High inflation and rising coin prices found investors pouring into the hobby by the tens of thousands.

These photos (opposite page) show the difference in grade between a Morgan silver dollar that is in mint state (uncirculated) condition (left) and one that is in well-circulated condition. Note the amount of design details that are present on the uncirculated example. The final grade is one of the most important factors in determining the value of a coin.

Twenty Cents (Barber)	1875–1878
Quarter Dollar	1796–date
Draped Bust/ Sm. Eagle (Scot)	1796
Draped Bust/ Lg. Eagle (Scot)	1804–1807
Capped Bust (Reich, Kneass)	1815–1838
Liberty Seated (Gobrecht)	1838–1891
Liberty Head (Barber)	1892–1916
Standing Liberty (MacNeil)	1916–1930
Washington (Silver) (Flanagan)	1932–1964
Washington (Clad) (Flanagan)	1965–date
Bicentennial rev. (Ahr)	1976

The descriptive grading system was simply too personal for them. They wanted a solid quantitative system that anyone could apply to any coin.

In addition, investors really weren't interested in the lower-grade coins. They were interested in making money and the way to do that was to buy the top grades. These appreciated faster and went higher. Thus, demand for uncirculated coins increased enormously while demand for lesser grades (Fine and Good) remained stagnant. What was needed was a grading system that expanded the upper ranges.

In an attempt to do this, the hobby adopted a grading system introduced by William Sheldon, M.D., in 1949 that was originally aimed strictly at early American cents. Dr. Sheldon reasoned that a coin's condition was determined by how close it was to the original mint state. Therefore, why not assign numbers indicating its relative position?

Dr. Sheldon's system consisted of the numbers 70 to 1. Grade 70 represented true, perfect mint condition. Grade 1 was the lowest possible, reserved for hunks of metal with virtually no discernible design or lettering.

Collectors, through the offices of the American Numismatic Association, modified Dr. Sheldon's original scale and blended it with the earlier descriptive scale. The new Mint State or MS, scale currently in use reads as follows:

DESCRIPTION	MINT STATE
Perfect	MS-70
Choice Uncirculated	MS-65
Uncirculated	MS-60
Choice About Uncirculated	AU-55
About Uncirculated	AU-50
Extremely Fine	EF-40
Very Fine	VF-20
Fine	F-12
Very Good	VG-8
Good	G-4
About Good	AG-3

U.S. 1866 shield nickel. It wasn't until the advent of this coin that a five cent piece was called a nickel (because of the metal from which the coin is made). Prior to this date, five cent coins were made of silver, and were called half dimes.

Several other intermediate grades are used, as well, to describe a coin that is better than its base grade, but not quite nice enough to warrant a higher technical grade. These might include designations such as F-15, EF-45, and others, and take into account a concept known as "eye appeal"—how aesthetically pleasing a particular coin is to the viewer.

UNDERSTANDING THE GRADES

It's important to understand that these grades are to be used only by highly experienced coin collectors and dealers. Most newcomers to the hobby are quite surprised

U.S. 1920 Pilgrim tercentenary commemorative half dollar.

when they see, for example, an MS-65 coin compared to an AU-55. They simply can't tell the difference, because it takes a good eye and great knowledge to discern the differences. Telling the difference between an MS-60 and MS-65 is even harder.

The MS grading system was quickly embraced by all elements of the hobby from collectors to dealers to investors. However, it soon became apparent that it, too, had drawbacks. Investors demanded only top-flight material, that which graded MS-60 or higher. However, as a practical matter there were almost no coins which graded MS-70. Almost everything was either MS-60 or MS-65 or *somewhere in between.*

U.S. 1866 Liberty seated half dollar.

As a result of the need for more investment grades, in 1986 the American Numismatic Association adopted new grading guidelines for uncirculated coins. Now there are additional grades as follows: MS-60; MS-61; MS-62; MS-63; MS-64; MS-65; MS-66; MS-67; MS-68; MS-69; MS-70.

In addition the ANA also produced descriptive terms for each grade (not included here because of their complexity). However, rather than produce solutions, these new grades only produced arguments and more problems.

As noted above, the average person cannot tell the difference between an MS-65 and an AU-55. How then, can they tell the difference, for example, between an MS-65

U.S. 1876 twenty cent piece. A very short-lived denomination (1875-1878), it was very unpopular because of its similarity in both size and design to the then-circulating quarter dollar. A similar fate, and for similar reasons, befell the Susan B. Anthony dollar, which was minted for only a few years.

and an MS-64? Many dealers, at the time, contended that even they could not make the distinction!

Further, the number of coins above MS-65 were extremely limited. Thus a kind of hobby warfare started. One person might argue that this coin was MS-64 while another argued it was only MS-63.

MONEY RULES

While at first it may seem like it was a trivial pursuit to worry about the differences between grades that are so close together, in actual fact what was at stake was millions of dollars. That is serious money and hence the deep

U.S. 1875 Liberty seated quarter dollar. Coins were made of silver, and were called half dimes.

concern over grading.

The money came into play because large investors wanted to buy only the top grades. They wanted to buy only MS-65 coins. This meant that, for example, an 1885 silver dollar in MS-65 condition might sell for $285. However, the same coin in MS-63 condition would only bring $30. Note, we're talking about so slight a difference that many dealers could not tell the coins apart.

The desire to grade coins MS-65 in order to get the most money for them often overtook reality. Hence, many coins were overgraded. Coins that were in reality MS-63s or even MS-60s, were given higher grades. Investors only learned the truth when it came time to sell and their

U.S. 1835 capped bust half dime.

$10,000 coin turned out to be worth only $500.

What was needed was some authority to say that this was the official grade. What was needed was a coin-grading service with an unblemished reputation. And coin professionals responded to the need.

ANACS

The first attempt at coin grading was done by the American Numismatic Association Certification Service, an arm of the ANA. Created in the early 1970s, this organization set out not to grade coins but instead to cer-

U.S. 1893 Isabella commemorative quarter dollar. Struck in Chicago during the World's Columbian Exposition, these coins were sold as souvenirs for $1 each. They hold the distinction of being the only domestic coins struck by the U.S. Mint to bear the portrait of a foreign monarch (Queen Isabella of Spain, patron of Christopher Columbus).

tify that they were authentic and not counterfeits. (At the time the hobby had been suffering from a plague of counterfeit pieces.)

By the early 1980s, however, the ANA decided to expand ANACS's services to include grading coins. This move was universally applauded, as it would bring homogeneity to what was a wildly diffuse hobby. However, things didn't turn out quite as planned.

ANACS suffered from several drawbacks. One was that the service catered mainly to the hobby, not to investors. Hence, it gave more attention to "technical" grading and less to investor grading which would have taken "eye appeal" into account. Investors were interested in such

U.S. 1795 flowing hair type silver dollar. The earliest type of silver dollar to be struck under the authority of the U.S. government at its national mint, these coins gained immediate acceptance as legal tender by the public. This design was used only during 1794 and 1795.

things as "strike," or the sharpness of the design, and "luster," or the brightness of the coin. ANACS, on the other hand, seemed interested more in how well the coin had been preserved. Almost immediately dealers began balking at the grades ANACS was handing out, saying they were too low or too inconsistent.

Secondly, ANACS returned the coins with a picture and a certificate. It was possible, however, for an unscrupulous seller to substitute a coin of a lesser grade. An unwary buyer might purchase a certificated coin not realizing that the certificate didn't match the coin. It took a very experienced eye to be able to tell whether or not the coin in the photo was actually the coin in hand.

U.S. 1859 Liberty seated dime.

Finally, in the mid-1980s, demand for grading grew to the point where ANACS simply could not handle the load. As a result, ANACS was overwhelmed and those submitting coins sometimes had to wait months for their certificates. This was an impossible situation for dealers whose livelihood depended on quickly turning around coin sales.

PRIVATE COIN CERTIFICATES

In response to this problem, in the late 1980s, several large coin dealers decided to create their own certification services. Most well-known among these are the Profes-

Very rare and popular five pound gold piece, issued by Great Britain in 1839, shortly after Queen Victoria ascended the throne. Known as the ''Una and the lion'' piece because of its reverse design, it is one of the classic collectors' coins of the world.

sional Coin Grading Service (PCGS), and the Numismatic Guaranty Corporation of America (NGCA). Other such services included the Numismatic Certification Institute (NCI), International Numismatic Society (INS), and many others. At one time, almost every large dealer in the country was starting his own competitive grading service. Many of these grading services would only accept coins from dealers. And some services were composed of dealers around the country sworn to honor the grade given.

A new twist that these dealers added was to encase the coins they graded in plastic. When a coin was returned from a grading service, both the certificate and the coin were in a slab of plastic. Hence, these graded coins became known as slabs. The idea was that this way a coin of a lesser grade could not be substituted with the certificate.

These private grading services have far outdistanced ANACS in the number of coins graded, the speed of the grading and, in some cases, the reputation of the grades delivered. They have gone a very long way toward quantifying the hobby.

PROBLEMS WITH SLABS

It must be pointed out, however, that simply because a coin has been graded by a service and is encased in plastic with a certificate stating its grade, the coin hasn't necessarily been accurately graded. Some grading services were notoriously lax in their standards. Others remained strict. And over time, the lax services sometimes tightened up while the strict ones became looser.

Therefore, today dealers will buy coins on the basis not only of a grade given by the certificate, but by whom the certificate is from. Some grading services were so notoriously lax that their coins graded, for example, between 1987 and 1990 might only be worth 40 percent of normal market value for their grade!

When buying slabs, it is not enough to simply have the grade on a certificate. You must also know the reputation of the grading company for the year the grade was given. Any large, reputable dealer can supply you with this information. (You may want to check with several dealers to confirm it.)

ENTER THE BIG MONEY

Starting in 1988, Wall Street took notice of the grading that was occurring in rare coins and decided there was money to be made. Hence, several of the largest firms began creating partnerships for the purpose of buying rare coins, holding them, and then reselling them later for large profits.

Half Dollar	1794–date
Flowing Hair (Scot)	1794–1795
Draped Bust/ Sm. Eagle (Scot)	1796–1797
Draped Bust/ Lg. Eagle (Scot)	1801–1807
Capped Bust Reeded Edge (Gobrecht)	1836–1839
Liberty Seated (Gobrecht)	1839–1891
Liberty Head (Barber)	1892–1915
Liberty Walking (Weinman)	1916–1947
Franklin (Sinnock)	1948–1963
Kennedy (Silver) (Roberts, Gasparro)	1964
Kennedy (40% Silver) (Roberts, Gasparro)	1965–1970
Kennedy (Clad) (Roberts, Gasparro)	1971–date
Bicentennial rev. (Huntington)	1976

Today hundreds of million of dollars are pouring into the hobby from these very large acquisitions. The result of this is to drive the price of top-quality coins even higher.

THE ROLE OF THE COLLECTOR

In the face of all this "big money," what is a collector, one who is interested in collecting coins, not just investing in them, to do? The role of the collector in today's world of coins has changed significantly.

This is not to say, of course, that collectors are not interested in making a profit. I have never met anyone who wouldn't turn an eye toward the chance of profiting from a rare-coin collection. It is sad to say, however, that the collector is not necessarily in the mainstream of the field any longer. In fact, today rare-coin collecting seems to be divided into two separate areas. On the one hand are the investors and the large dealers who are in the field solely to make a profit and really don't have an interest in coins. On the other are the collectors whose primary goal is the same as that of the ancient Greeks and Romans who saved coins—to acquire a beautiful and historical treasure.

Today, the collector in the U.S. often no longer aims for the top grade of coin, since in many cases he simply cannot afford it. He does, however, aim just below the top grade.

As noted above, while the prices paid for MS-65 coins are astronomical, those paid for MS-60s and lower are quite reasonable. Today it is still possible to acquire an exciting, extensive, and comprehensive collection of American coins for a reasonable price, as long as you are willing to go just below the top.

The major coin publications realize this. A few years ago, *COINage* began publishing its Coin Price Index, or CPA, which was a composite average of the prices of 20 leading coins. However, in the late 1980s, this publication realized that the coins making up its index were really

U.S. 1986 one ounce silver bullion coin, $1 face value.

out of reach for most collectors. Hence it expanded its composite list and began a second index.

This second index is for coins in VF or Very Fine (VF-20) condition. These are low-priced coins that almost anyone can afford. To this day it runs two separate lists, one of MS-65 grade coins of interest primarily to investors, and one of low-priced coins that are of interest to collectors. *Coin World,* the leading weekly coin newspaper, has taken a similar tack.

In short, if you want to start out small, say with a hundred dollars or less, there's a whole wonderful hobby waiting for you. There are thousands of lesser-grade coins that

U.S. 1882 Indian head cent. A popular collectors' coin. Good condition common date examples can be purchased for under one dollar each.

will help make a marvelous collection.

But, many would-be collectors may point out, what about the profit angle? Sure, I want to start a collection and start small, but I want it to build. What chance is there for it to build when all the appreciation is taking place in the top-quality coins?

GRADING DRIFT

One answer to this is that even the lower-priced coins tend to appreciate in value over time, although certainly not nearly as fast as the higher-priced ones. Another answer has to do with "grading drift."

U.S. 1948 Franklin half dollar. This design was the predecessor of the Kennedy half dollar, and features a representation of the liberty bell on the reverse.

Grading drift means that the way a coin is graded has something to do with *when* it's graded. During periods when top coin prices are stagnant or even declining (yes, they do occasionally decline), there is a tendency to be very tough on grading. At these times there is a large supply of top-quality material and the grading services try very hard to be strict.

However, when the market explodes upward (as it has done), then there is a shortage of top-flight material (since everyone wants it) and the tendency is to be less strict in grading. As a result, during these "hot" periods coin grades tend to "advance." Material that in slower periods might have been graded as AU-55 gets advanced to

MS-60. MS-60 material might move up to MS-63, and so forth.

Thus, for a collector who studies the hobby and learns a great deal about the coins, the opportunity exists to make big profits without having to buy very expensive top-grade coins. What you need to do is to buy almost top-grade coins and then hope that during hot periods, your coins will advance a grade.

GRADING ADVANCEMENT WITH SLABBED COINS

Slabbed coins advance as well as those which are not certificated. For example, I recently saw one dealer who was offered some Arkansas Commemorative series half-dollars for $300 in MS-60 condition but not slabbed. He refused, saying he had no one to resell them to.

The owner then sent the coins into a grading service and received back grades of MS-64 and MS-65. Armed with the coins now in slabs with the grading certificates enclosed, the seller went back to the same dealer who bought the coins for $1,700! (There were the exact same coins he had earlier refused for $300 without certificates.)

The slab/certificate game is much like the old story of sardines in advertising. An advertising company was asked to create a campaign for canned sardines. A large number of cans of sardines appeared at the agency and the executives looked at them and thought hard until they came up with an idea to present to the client. The client liked it and they moved forward. In the meantime, a mail-boy at the agency came upon one of the cans and, being hungry, opened it. To his surprise he found it was empty. He called this to the attention of the account executive who smiled paternally and said, "Son, these sardines aren't for eating. These are for selling."

AMERICAN SILVER
COINS AND MEDALS

U.S. 1943 Liberty walking half dollar. Considered by many to be the most beautiful silver coin minted by the United States.

Most of what collectors of United States coins acquire is silver. Of course, there are the copper cents, nickel pieces, and gold coins (covered in the next chapter) for more specialized collectors. And then there's the clad coinage of the last few decades, which tends to be too recent, in most cases, to be worth collecting. That leaves silver.

Silver coinage was authorized by the new American Congress in 1792. It took two years, however, before the mint was able to produce the first coins. These were a beautiful Flowing Hair dollar, half-dollar and half-dime. (The half-dime should not be confused with the nickel. The half-dime was made of silver.) The purity of silver in

U.S. 1858 Liberty seated half dime. The original denomination of the five cent coin.

each piece was .892 (or 89.2 percent silver, 10.8 percent copper). This was changed in 1837 to the standard .900 fine (90 percent silver, 10 percent copper). These early coins were produced in limited numbers because of the lack of silver available to the mint. Today they are all considered quite valuable.

In the mid-1960s the price of silver rose to the point where, in some cases, the silver in a coin was worth more than the face value of the coin itself. As a result, investors began obtaining large numbers of the coins and melting them down for their silver content. This took silver coins out of circulation and produced the famous "coin shortage." The government blamed the shortage on collectors.

U.S. 1944 winged Liberty head, or "Mercury" dime. Circulated specimens can be bought for under one dollar.

In truth, the devaluation of the dollar was the cause.

During the period of the coin melt, vast numbers of silver coins were lost through melting. This has thrown off collectors in their search for rare coins. Some coins which were minted in the hundreds of millions have turned out to be in short supply because so many were melted down. In any event, the result was the elimination of silver coinage and the introduction of clad coinage in 1965. These clad coins were virtually worthless. They were true fiat currency (value dictated by government decree).

Once again in 1979 and 1980, when the price of silver temporarily rose to $50 an ounce, a melt-down occurred. Then, bags of silver coins that had not been melted in the

U.S. 1932 Washington quarter dollar. Originally struck in 1932 to commemorate the 200th anniversary of the birth of George Washington, the design proved so popular that it is still in use today. With the exception of a few key dates, these silver coins are well within the price range of the beginning collector.

mid-1960s, because of their numismatic value, suddenly were discovered to be worth more (because of silver's very high price) as bullion. Many millions of numismatically valued coins were destroyed in this second melt-down.

As a result of all this, there is a kind of black hole in all of the silver series from between about 1920 to 1964. Coins minted before 1920 were generally too numismatically valuable to be melted down. However, between those dates, coins were frequently not sufficiently valuable to withstand melting. In the future we may find the values of silver coins of this period escalating if it turns out that far fewer are left than collectors suspect.

Now, let's consider the silver coins themselves.

U.S. 1937-D Oregon Trail memorial commemorative half dollar.

HALF-DIMES First produced in 1794 with the Flowing Hair design, by 1796 the design changed. The half-dime produced from 1794 to 1873 took on a Draped Bust, then a Capped Bust and finally, in 1837, a Seated Liberty. These coins were produced in large numbers, frequently more than a million a year, and they are readily available to collectors in the lower grades. There are relatively few of these in MS-60 or higher grade and these command many hundreds of dollars, even for common dates.

DIMES Silver dimes have been produced since 1796. They have incorporated many designs, including a Draped Bust, Capped Bust, Liberty Seated, Liberty Head (designed by Charles Barber), and the famous Winged Liberty or Mercury dime designed by Adolph A. Weinman in 1916.

The Mercs (1916-1945) have always been the most popular of this denomination and, interestingly enough, many are still available for a reasonable price. (Depending on date and condition, Mercs can be found for less than $10.)

QUARTERS The history of the quarter mimics that of the dime. There have been many designs, including a Liberty Head designed by Charles Barber in 1892. But, the design that we all recognize is the Washington bust. This coin, with the eagle with outstretched wings on the reverse, is the most well known of American coins.

Produced since 1932, the coin used to be shunned by collectors as being too recent to be of numismatic value. Lately, however, some of the early quarters have earned the attention of collectors. In particular, those quarters produced between 1932 and 1964 that were made out of silver have caught collectors' attention. Collections featuring the entire series have sprung up and prices have increased. You can still get these coins for very little, but today's prices may seem like bargains in just a few years.

U.S. 1950-D Booker T. Washington memorial commemorative half dollar. Issued to perpetuate the ideals and teachings of this famous black American who was the founder of, and driving force behind, Tuskegee Institute.

The quarter was also produced in 1976 with a bicentennial reverse side. A few were minted in silver. Many people saved these pieces; however, to date they have not become highly valued, even in the silver issue.

HALF-DOLLARS The most popular half dollar coin ever designed was the Kennedy obverse. They were first minted in 1964 of .900 fine (90% pure) silver, and from 1965 through 1970 contained a net amount of .400 fine (or 40% pure) silver in a clad, or "sandwich" composition (beginning in 1971, they contained no silver at all). Although hundreds and hundreds of millions of these coins were produced in silver, you will not find a single one in circulation today. They were all removed and either

PRIVATE ISSUE SILVER

In addition to the silver coins issued by the U.S. Mint, there are numerous private issues. These have become increasingly popular over the past three decades.

It's important to remember, however, that only an official mint issues "coins" (coinage of the realm—money). Everything else is a medal, no matter how it may be advertised.

The interest in private-issued medals was spurred on by the private Franklin Mint in the late 1960s and through the 1970s. The Franklin Mint issues were of almost pure silver and had marvelous designs. In addition, the strikes were of proof quality—that is, they were superb. (The Franklin Mint even had a special "clean room" where the workers wore special clothing, gloves, and face masks in order to produce the highest-quality pieces.)

Many people across the country bought these Franklin Mint and other mint medals not only for their beauty, but as a way to invest in silver. However, by the late 1970s, the bloom was off many of these issues. They were initially sold for substantially more than the price of silver and so many were issued that they never seemed to rise in value.

The silver boom of 1979 and 1980 put an end to this concern. The rising price of silver made the original Franklin Mint and similar medals worth many times their original purchase price. Those who were wise enough sold before the price of silver collapsed.

In the 1980s many new private mints issuing their own designs came into existence. Some of these skyrocketed in value as collectors sought to get hold of the pieces. Among the most popular were a series based on the Walt Disney characters Snow White and Mickey Mouse. At one point, medals that were issued with these designs were selling for $500 and more.

Overall, non-mint produced medals are of questionable collector value. A few tend to sell very well, but the vast majority rarely exceed the price originally asked for them. Additionally, the value of these pieces is closely linked to the price of silver. As the value of silver has gone down in recent years, so too has the popularity of these pieces.

melted down for their silver content in 1979 and 1980 or stored away by collectors. Today, even though these coins are only about twenty years old, they command prices considerably above face value.

In 1976 a special commemorative Kennedy half was issued both in copper-nickel clad and in about 40 percent silver. Once again the silver coins were strictly intended for collectors. However, so many of them were produced (about 15 million) that their prices even today are quite modest.

DOLLAR   The dollar, like the other silver coins, has a long and colorful history. A wide variety of Liberties, both seated and shown in bust only have been featured. A slightly heavier, silver trade dollar for export was produced at one point.

Probably the most popular silver dollar ever designed is the Liberty head or "Morgan" type, issued from 1878 until 1921. But another popular design is the peace type issued between 1921 and 1935. Designed by Anthony De Francisci, actually a medalist by profession, this coin features a stylized liberty or peace head on the obverse and a standing eagle on the reverse. The design was originally in high relief (making it stand out from the coin). This, however, made it impractical for minting and its relief was reduced.

When people speak of a "silver dollar," frequently what they are thinking of is this peace design. You won't, however, find this silver dollar in change. The silver in the coin long ago became far more valuable than the face value of the piece. Today peace and other silver dollars are either held by collectors and investors or have been melted down.

Between 1971 and 1978 the United States issued an Eisenhower dollar. This featured President Eisenhower on the obverse and an eagle landing on the moon (to symbolize America's efforts in space) on the reverse.

U.S. 1979-D Susan B. Anthony dollar.

The Ike dollars were issued in silver as well as copper-nickel, with the silver coins intended for collectors. However, the design by Frank Gasparro was widely criticized, especially the "bump" apparent at the top of Eisenhower's head. Although nearly half a billion of the coins were struck in copper-nickel, they are no longer found in circulation. Most have been melted down over the years, although some are being held by collectors.

The most reviled American coin was the Susan B. Anthony dollar. First struck in 1979, this coin featured a somewhat unimaginative bust of the famous suffragette on the obverse and the same reverse as the Ike dollar. The coin was "down-sized" and was shunned by the public, who felt it was too similar in diameter to a quarter. Some people condemned the coin because its small size seemed to reflect the reduced buying power of the dollar. Others just hated the design. Although great numbers were produced, the coin circulated for only three years.

Today the coin of choice for many investors (who are not collectors) is the silver dollar. In fact, silver dollars of the 1800s in MS-60 or higher condition have almost become the "only" coin that some investors will buy.

NICKEL Although issued primarily in a nickel-copper alloy, this coin was issued briefly in silver (.350, or 35 percent pure) during the Second World War (1942-1945) when nickel was in short supply. These wartime silver nickels tended to quickly tarnish and fade. Those in circulation were discarded after the war. However, many in pristine condition remain in collections, and they reflect light with a marvelous silver sheen.

The most popular American coin ever comes from this series even though it wasn't minted in silver. It is the Indian Head or buffalo nickel. Issued between 1913 and 1938, it includes many varieties (such as a buffalo shown with only three legs—1937D—caused by an overpolished die. All these unusual strikes only add to the interest of the coin.

The buffalo design was by James E. Fraser, a famous sculptor and artist of western subjects. He reputedly used the faces of three Indians to create the obverse and the buffalo (named Black Diamond) at the New York Zoological Gardens for the reverse.

For generations, young collectors entered the hobby by collecting buffalo nickels right along with their Lincoln cent books. The design was so striking, however, that the buffalo nickel was always the more popular.

U.S. 1936 buffalo or Indian head nickel (above, left); U.S. 1937-D buffalo nickel (above, right). The so-called three-legged variety, created when the die that struck these coins was overly polished, causing some of the detail (including one of the buffalo's legs) to be ground away.

SPECIAL ISSUE COINS

A word should be mentioned about silver coins issued by official mints for collectors.

These collector issues, particularly those from mints, outside North America, often might best be termed *export coins*. They are coins that are "officially" produced, but even though they are intended strictly for collectors, they may lack collector value because they were never meant for circulation. For example, the Isle of Man in the past has issued a large number of official coins that seem to have more distribution in America than their homeland.

These are often beautiful and appealing, but they haven't passed the test of time. Coins issued by the United States Mint may fit this category as well.

What this usually means is that these pieces haven't been around for fifty years or more so that collectors can determine whether or not they will be worth acquiring. In general, silver coins that are issued strictly for collectors by mints may or may not ultimately be valued. A lot depends on the coins themselves. If they are simultaneously issued for wide circulation and if they happen to be a key coin (one that's necessary to fill out a set) or if they have an error or some other peculiar feature, then they may be valuable.

But the key point to understand is that collector coins issued by mints are not necessarily the best collectibles. Mints, government as well as private, do not determine what collectors will acquire and what will become rare and valuable. Only collectors do that.

Collecting American Gold Coins

U.S. 1896 Liberty head double eagle, or $20 gold.

Acquiring American gold coins has become popular for both investors and collectors. However, because gold is expensive, collecting these coins tends to be a costly pursuit. Nevertheless, those who do collect these treasures are often amply rewarded monetarily and aesthetically. Before you learn about specific American gold pieces that you might want to collect, you should understand just how gold coins are valued. Unlike with their silver counterparts, the value of the metal itself comes heavily into play here.

Even a common date, poor condition gold coin is going to be costly. For example, if we're talking about a twenty-dollar gold piece (called a double-eagle), one of the most

U.S. 1924 St. Gaudens double eagle, or $20 gold. The "lower relief" type issued from 1907 to 1933.

common gold coins available, in a condition well below investor grade, we're still speaking of nearly an ounce of pure gold. The gold in the coin itself, without considering any numismatic value, is worth the current market value for gold bullion. If gold happens to be selling for $400 an ounce at the time (the price fluctuates, but we'll just use $400 as an arbitrary figure), the coin is worth $400.

But, since gold United States coins are highly prized no matter what their condition is, the coin is actually worth more than the value of the gold. The coin bears a premium for its numismatic or collector value. The premium could boost its price up several hundred dollars or more. (The premium varies depending on the market demand

Dollar	1794–1981
Flowing Hair (Scot)	1794–1795
Draped Bust/ Sm. Eagle (Scot)	1795–1798
Draped Bust/ Lg. Eagle (Scot)	1798–1804
Liberty Seated (Gobrecht)	1836–1873
Flying Eagle rev. (Gobrecht)	1836–1839
Liberty Head (Morgan)	1878–1921
Peace (DeFrancisci)	1921–1935
Eisenhower (Clad) (Gasparro)	1971–1978
Eisenhower, 40% Sil. (Gasparro)	1971–1974
Bicentennial rev. (Williams)	1976
Susan B. Anthony (Gasparro)	1979–1981
Trade Dollar (Barber)	1873–1885

for the coins. If bullion prices are rising, the numismatic premium will rise, often to several hundred dollars a coin. If gold prices are falling, so too will the numismatic premium.

Thus many investors buy old United States gold coins as a means of investing in gold bullion. You yourself, even though your inclination may be more toward collecting, may find it worthwhile to spend some of your money on common gold coins, particularly when the market's going up.

RARE GOLD COINS

Interestingly enough, very rare gold coins behave in a fashion similar to common date gold coins. Logic would suggest that a rare gold coin, one in investor condition and/or of a rare date, would not be affected by the price of bullion. After all, such a rare double-eagle might be worth $10,000 or more. In such a coin the value of the intrinsic gold is less than five percent of the numismatic value of the coin.

Yet, when gold is hot and bullion prices are rising, the value of rare gold coins goes up as well. Similarly when gold prices fall, so do the values of the rare gold coins. It would seem that the activity of the gold bullion market is reflected in the popularity of even the rarest gold coins.

UNDERSTANDING THE GOLD MARKET

At least a cursory understanding of the gold bullion market is necessary for anyone who is going to collect gold coins. (Not understanding the market can leave you open to some rather harsh surprises.) Gold, as stated in the first chapters, was a monetary metal dating back to the earliest coins, and the United States produced gold coins as early as 1795. These early gold coins were the accepted means of owning gold bullion and in those days,

U.S. 1878 $3 gold. Another odd denomination coin whose only reason for existence was that its value equaled the purchase price of 100 postage stamps.

the value of the coin was determined completely by the quantity of the gold bullion it contained. (Bullion means gold in the form of bars, refined, but not minted into coins.)

In the nineteenth century United States gold coins competed with the gold money of other countries such as England. It wasn't until this century that United States dominance of gold appeared.

As noted earlier, during the dark days of the Great Depression, President Roosevelt was faced with a crisis of deflation. So many banks had gone bankrupt that people no longer trusted them. Instead, they hid their money in their mattresses or buried it in the ground. And the

Gold Coins	
One Dollar Gold	1849–1889
Quarter Eagle ($2.50 Gold)	1796–1929
Three Dollar Gold	1854–1889
Half Eagle ($5.00 Gold)	1795–1929
Eagle ($10.00 Gold)	1795–1933
Double Eagle ($20.00 Gold)	1849–1933
Private and Territorial Gold Coins struck in the United States (Georgia, North Carolina, California, Oregon, Utah, and Colorado)	1830–1861
U.S. Commemorative Coinage	1893–date
Gold and Silver Bullion Coins	1986–date
Era of Modern Collectors	1920–date

money that was considered most valuable was gold coins. Roosevelt had to get that money back into circulation in order to start the economy moving again.

So, in 1933 he decreed that all gold coins (with the exception of rare numismatic gold) were to be turned in and melted. An enormous amount of gold coinage was returned to the government and converted into gold bars. As noted earlier, this forms the majority of the American stockpile of gold.

He also fixed the price of gold at $35 an ounce (from the previous value of $20.67 an ounce, thereby devaluing the American dollar by nearly 70%), and agreed to buy back United States currency from foreign governments at the rate of 35 paper dollars for each ounce of gold.

By the end of the 1930s, however, Europe was at war, and England in particular was facing an economic crisis into which gold figured heavily. The war effort had drained the British monetary reserves. Therefore, the United States began accepting British gold in payment for materials sent overseas. It did the same thing with currencies of other countries immediately after the war.

As a result, by 1946 the United States had stockpiled the greatest reserves of gold the world had ever seen. Further, since the dollar was backed (at least partly) by gold, the dollar became the strongest currency on earth. For a good ten years nothing challenged the supremacy of United States gold and paper money.

By the late 1950s, however, European countries were making a strong comeback and the United States was finding that its dollar was weakening. For the first time in decades, the United States began to ship gold overseas in order to buy back United States paper money and to keep the dollar's value up.

In 1961 this outflow of gold became alarming and the United States government extended its prohibition on private ownership of gold by United States citizens in foreign countries as well as at home. Foreign countries and cen-

U.S. 1873 gold dollar. This denomination was first minted in 1849 after the California gold discoveries brought large quantities of that metal into the U.S. economy.

tral banks continued to erode our stockpile of gold by demanding the precious metal in exchange for United States paper currency they held, and by the 1970s our gold reserves had been cut virtually in half. To try and stem this tremendous drain, the United States raised its official exchange rate to $38 per ounce in 1972, and to $42.22 per ounce in 1973. Then, in an unprecedented move, it took the United States off the gold standard and allowed the dollar to float relative to other currencies. In 1975 it lifted all restrictions against gold ownership for United States citizens. Today you can own as much gold as you want in any form.

As a result, since 1973 the United States gold reserves have not appreciably declined. Whereas prior to that time gold was strictly a commodity of exchange between governments, in 1975 it became a commodity to be exchanged between private citizens. The price of gold now fluctuates on the open market largely unaffected by the actions of the United States and other western governments.

WHAT AFFECTS THE PRICE OF GOLD TODAY?

Today, the price of gold and its influence on collectible gold coins is largely determined by five factors:

1. The quantity produced by mining
2. The rate of inflation
3. The perspective of investors
4. World crisis
5. Dumping by Russia

MINING More gold is being mined today than ever before in history. Each year the production of gold in this country is higher than the year before. Although gold production in South Africa (the world's largest producer) is down as its mines peter out after a century of production, the slack has more than been taken up by the United States and other gold producers.

INFLATION Gold is widely perceived as a hedge against inflation. When inflation rises, gold prices almost always go up. When the United States had an inflation rate of 12 percent in 1980, gold topped out at $840 an ounce.

INVESTORS' PERSPECTIVE Some investors see gold as a good place to store money. From 1975 until

U.S. private and territorial gold $5 issue of Christopher Bechtler. Rutherford County, North Carolina, was this country's principal supplier of mined gold from 1790 until the 1840s, and this gold was assayed, refined, and minted into coins at the source by private individuals in order to facilitate counting and shipping, as well as to provide a much-needed medium of exchange for local merchants.

1985, United States investors were the biggest buyers of gold. But after that, as Americans became disenchanted with gold because of price drops, Japanese investors took over. From about 1986 until 1989 the Japanese, who had just been given permission to own gold, bought huge quantities of it. But, when prices did not push high, they too became disenchanted.

One point is worth noting. The Japanese have been interested only in .999 (99.9 percent) fine or pure gold whereas most American gold has been either .900 (90 percent) or .9167 (91.67 percent or 22 karat) fine. Thus, American gold coins have held no allure for the Japanese.

WORLD CRISIS During periods of world crisis, such as the war in Iran and Iraq or the Soviet invasion of Afghanistan, gold prices tend to rise. Investors as well as average citizens remember that the precious metal has been the ultimate form of money since ancient times and, as a consequence, seek it out when peace is threatened.

DUMPING BY RUSSIA The Soviet Union is the second largest gold producer in the world. It uses its gold, however, as a means of obtaining hard currency on the world markets. (The Russian ruble is considered virtually worthless, so to buy American grain or German computers, the Soviet Union must sell gold.) Russia's sales, however, are not timed to coincide with market conditions. When the Soviets need hard currency, they sell gold. If the market happens to be down at the time, Russia's sales can depress it further. If the market happens to be up, they have little effect on it.

Thus the gold market waxes and wanes and, correspondingly, so do the prices of U.S. gold coins. If you're going to invest in U.S. gold, you would be well advised to keep an eye on the price of gold and on the five factors that influence that price.

UNITED STATES GOLD COINS

$20 GOLD As noted, the most well-known U.S. gold pieces are the double eagles, or $20 gold. They were minted from 1849 until Roosevelt cut off private gold ownership in 1933. They were made from an alloy of 90 percent gold and 10 percent copper (the copper being added to improve the wearing ability of the coin), and contained .9676 ounce of pure gold. Thus, at a price of $20.67 per ounce, the gold in a double eagle was worth exactly $20.

The early coins featured a Liberty Head and are considered to be rare collector's issues, even in the poorest condition. However, coins in all grades but MS-60 and higher dated after about 1860 can generally be obtained for the bullion price of gold plus a premium as noted above.

There were two distinct varieties of the 1907 coins made: one struck in a high, almost medallic, relief and with the date in Roman numerals; the second in a lower relief with date in Arabic numerals. Very few high relief coins were produced, and their prices tend to be very high. Several dates in the series can be purchased for bullion plus a premium, although many dates can be very expensive. The 1927-D, for example, sells for well over $100,000. (Although nearly half a million coins were struck bearing the 1933 date, none were officially released into circulation by the government, and although a few somehow found their way out of the mint, it is, nevertheless, illegal to possess them.)

$10 GOLD These Eagles were first minted in 1795 and the earliest coins featured a capped bust on the obverse and a poorly designed eagle that some have referred to as a chicken on the reverse. Because of the age of these coins, those issued until 1804 are considered quite rare and regularly command prices into five figures.

U.S. 1907 St. Gaudens double eagle, or $20 gold. Struck in high (almost medallic) relief with Roman numerals used for the date, it was made in limited quantities during 1907 only. Feeling that our country's coinage lacked any expression of beauty or art, President Theodore Roosevelt commissioned the noted sculptor and artist, Augustus St. Gaudens, to design a coin that would reflect more interest in aesthetics. However, the intricate detail was difficult to achieve using the mint's high-speed coining presses, so bowing to the commercial needs of quantity rather than quality, the mint modified the design after only several thousand pieces had been struck. The resulting lower relief coins of 1907 and 1933 were beautiful, but not nearly as imposing as the high relief originals.

The coin was .9167 gold.

The design was changed several times, but the most famous was the Augustus St. Gaudens Indian head put into service in 1907. This famed Indian head coin became an American trademark, and no collector of United States gold would want to be without several. For almost all dates, they are available for the price of bullion plus a premium in all grades below MS-60.

SMALLER GOLD
The United States at various times also minted other gold coins. The half-eagle, or $5 gold, was minted from 1795 through 1929. It had various designs, but again the most famous was the incused

U.S. 1913 Indian head quarter eagle, or $2.50 gold (above, left). Struck from 1908 until 1929, this coin (along with the $5 gold of the same years) bears the distinction of being the only one made in this country where the design is struck ''incused,'' or into the surface of the coin, rather than being raised, or in ''relief,'' from it. A $50 octagonal private issue (also known as a ''slug'')

of Augustus Humbert, United States Assayer of Gold, California (above, right). These large, heavy gold ''coins'' were actually no more than fancy ingots, and served the purpose of facilitating the counting of large amounts of gold. The respected name of the assayer, stamped on the piece, assured that it contained the proper weight and fineness (therefore value) of gold.

(sunken) design of an Indian head by Bela Lyon Pratt from 1908 to 1929 that was also used for the quarter eagle. This coin was .900 fine gold.

The United States also minted a $3 gold piece (1854–1889), a quarter eagle, or $2.50 gold piece (1796–1929), and gold dollars (1849 to 1889). Many of these smaller pieces in common dates and in grades under MS-60 are readily available to collectors at reasonable prices.

TERRITORIAL GOLD

Mentioned earlier, territorial gold was struck in Georgia (Templeton Reid, 1830), North Carolina (Bechtler, 1830–1852), and extensively in San Francisco primarily during the 1850s gold rush era. These coins bear a wide range of designs and some are octagonal while others are little more than rectangular bars of gold with their minter and weight stamped onto them.

All of the territorial gold is treasured by a small but determined group of collectors who trade largely among themselves. Prices for most pieces are very high.

COMMEMORATIVE GOLD

From time to time, the United States has issued gold pieces to commemorate various events. These include the Louisiana Purchase Exposition dollars of 1903, the Lewis and Clark Exposition dollars of 1904 and 1905, the Grant Memorial dollars of 1922, and the famed Panama Pacific Exposition dollars of 1915 featuring the profile of a Canal builder. Surprisingly, almost all of these and others as well are available for a reasonable premium over their bullion price in conditions under MS-60.

BULLION COINS

In 1986 the United States government began minting American eagle bullion coins. The gold versions were struck in four sizes: one ounce ($50 face value), half ounce ($25), quarter ounce ($10), and tenth ounce ($5). The obverse design was adapted

U.S. 1903 Louisiana Purchase Exposition commemorative gold dollar. Issued for the exposition that was held in St. Louis.

U.S. 1986 one ounce gold American eagle bullion coin with a $50 face value.

from the St. Gaudens motif, and the reverse displayed a family of eagles. (A one ounce silver piece [$1 face value], featuring A.A. Weinman's walking Liberty design, was also produced.) They were designed to compete in the bullion market against the one ounce Canadian maple leaf and South African krugerrand.

Although the coins got off to a good start, the program has faltered in recent years. The main reason seems to be that the coins were issued in .9167 fine (22-karat) gold. However, as noted earlier, Asian buyers, primarily the Japanese, prefer pure gold or .999 fine such as the Canadian maple leaf. Hence, the United States coin has fared poorly. In 1986, their first full year, nearly two million eagles were sold. By 1989 that figure had dropped to only half a million.

Today, collectors usually include at least one of the eagles as part of their collection. Real gold buffs also include the other major gold bullion coins, which include the maple leaf, krugerrand, Australian nugget, and Chinese panda coins. (The early issues of panda coins from the mid-1980s have become quite rare and expensive.)

The American eagle sells for the price of bullion plus a small premium, usually around 5 percent. Part of that premium is recouped when the coin is ultimately resold.

COLLECTING GOLD

If you're a gold coin collector, it helps to have deep pockets. Because of the metal, the coins simply aren't cheap. However, even a collector of modest means can make an initial buy, and, by selling coins as they appreciate and investing the money in others, eventually build quite an enviable collection.

ERROR COINS, FAKES, AND COUNTERFEITS

Two different types of U.S. striking errors: The cent at left has been double-struck (the first strike normal, the second off-center, from not having been fully ejected from the coining press); at left, below, is an example of an off-center strike (caused when the blank planchet was not properly aligned between the dies at the time of striking).

As you begin collecting, particularly if you collect less than investment-grade coins (those that aren't "slabbed"), you run the risk of obtaining fake or counterfeit coins. On the other hand, sometimes a coin that looks strange may actually be a legitimate error piece and, for that reason, be more valuable. In this chapter we'll look both at error coins and at problem pieces.

ERROR COINS

A coining error occurs at the mint, not afterward. If you think of a mint as a manufacturing facility producing billions of little products annually, it is easy to see how mis-

Enlargement of the date area of the 1942-over-one U.S. Mercury dime, an example of what is known as an overdate error. Because of an error that occurred during the die manufacturing process, all coins struck by that particular die clearly show both a 2 and a 1 as the fourth digit in the date.

takes can occur. It is a testament to quality control that so few pieces actually escape detection, and this fact accounts for the rarity and value of those that do.

Error coins can take on many sizes, shapes, and types, but all fall within three distinct categories: *planchet errors* (something wrong with the disc of metal from which a coin is made); *die errors* (something wrong with the die that strikes the coin); and *striking errors* (something wrong that occurs at the exact time the coin is being struck in the coining press).

In modern minting techniques, obverse and reverse dies strike a planchet, or blank piece of metal, simultaneously from both sides. This is done under tremendous pressure, and the dies literally squeeze the planchet while imparting the design onto the face and back, creating the vertical lines we see on the edges of dimes, quarters, half dollars, and dollars. When something goes wrong at any time during the minting process, the resulting coin will sometimes be only a minor oddity, while at other times it will be something that looks quite spectacular, such as a copper quarter (one that was struck on a blank intended for a cent that inadvertently found its way into the quarter press).

Other errors include fragments (pieces of scrap metal that were struck by the dies), double strikes (coins that were struck a second time by the dies without having been pushed out of the press by the mechanism), and off-center strikes (planchets that were struck without first having been properly aligned between the dies). Yet other times a mint mark may be added or missing from the die. Let's consider some of the more famous error pieces.

Some 63 million 1916 Buffalo nickels were produced at the Philadelphia Mint alone. However, a few of these were struck with a doubled obverse die (one that had been manufactured improperly, with the result that all coins made from that particular die have the design elements doubled). The original collectors lucky enough to find these were rewarded by having a coin that was worth a hundred times the value of the normal 1916 Philadelphia pieces.

Something similar happened in 1955 to the Lincoln cent. Although more than 330 million of them were struck at the Philadelphia Mint, only a few hundred had the double-die error. Today the regular 1955 cent in MS-65 condition is worth perhaps a quarter. But the double die is worth hundreds of dollars.

Another type of error occurs when the mint tries to save money, or is in a hurry, and tries to reuse old dies. For example, during World War II, the mint accidently took a die for a 1941 dime and reimpressed it with the hub (a die is a negative image of a coin, while a hub is a positive image, and is used to make the die that will strike the

U.S. 1909-S VDB Lincoln head cent.

coin) that was to be used to make 1942 dies. The resulting coins struck by that die clearly show the "2" in the date stamped over a "1", creating what is called an "overdate" error. Again, this coin is many times more valuable than its properly-minted counterparts.

Varieties occur when minor design changes take place, while the overall coin remains substantially the same. The Lincoln cent was created by Victor David Brenner. Brenner insisted that his full name, "Brenner," be placed on the coin. The mint refused, saying that it would break a 70-year tradition, but agreed to put his initials "VDB" on the coin. After all, the then-circulating Indian head cent had its designer's (James B. Longacre)

U.S. 1955 Lincoln head cent. The famous doubled-die error. This error was caused when the die rotated slightly during its manufacturing process, causing a double image. That image was passed on to all the coins struck with that die.

initial ''L'' on it. So, his initials appeared at the bottom of the reverse of the first coins struck in 1909, the first year they were issued.

When the cent was released, though, there was a large protest since the initials (as small as they were) were more prominent than initials had been on previous coins. Newspaper editorials made great leaps of logic and contained references to Brenner's country of origin, Lithuania, then a monarchy. They reasoned that the initials were part of a plan to return monarchy to the United States! Still others attacked President Theodore Roosevelt, who was responsible for commissioning Brenner to design the coin, for somehow bestowing some kind of special treatment upon the artist. They wondered how could he be so utterly bold as to dictate his wishes and have them followed, without question, on our nation's money.

It was, of course, a tempest in a teapot. But the mint, bowing to pressure, removed the initials, meaning there were two varieties of Lincoln cents in 1909. Of the San Francisco Mint coins, those with the initials are several times scarcer and more costly than their non-initialed counterparts. The 1909-S VDB cent, key coin in the Lincoln series, has been the dream catch of many beginning collectors as they try to complete a set of Lincoln "pennies."

Other errors and varieties include weak strikes or "filled die" pieces, where the full design does not show even on high quality, mint state pieces. Yet others include engraving blunders and mismatched die pairs. The whole filed is constantly changing as new errors are discovered. Some collectors specialize in nothing else.

COUNTERFEITS

Counterfeiting has historical precedence going back to the ancient coins of Greece. In fact, as long as there have been coins, there have been counterfeiters. Most modern counterfeiting has taken the form of forging paper currency. For example, a counterfeiter might create plates to produce a phony $100 bill. However, modern counterfeiters have also produced phony coins, particularly the more rare and valuable ones.

For example, one area where counterfeiters have thrived is in adding mint marks. In the past the Philadelphia Mint produced coins without mint marks. On the other hand other mints, such as San Francisco, added mint marks to their coins, such as an S.

Earlier in this chapter we talked about the VDB cent. There were 27,995,000 of these coins produced at the Philadelphia Mint in 1909 without a mint mark. However, production was just getting started at San Francisco in 1909 so only 484,000 of them were produced. Thus the VDB cent with the S mint mark is worth hundreds of dollars in MS-60 condition while the same coin without the mint mark (from the Philadelphia Mint) is worth less than $20.

What some enterprising criminals have done is to buy legitimate 1909 VDB coins from the Philadelphia Mint and common-date cents from the San Francisco Mint (which aren't worth a great deal). Then they have removed the S mint mark from the common date San Francisco coin and soldered it onto the Philadelphia 1909-VDB coin producing a counterfeit 1909-S piece. They have then attempted to resell these coins for a huge profit.

This particular counterfeiting scheme is well known to dealers and most will examine any S mint mark under a high-power microscope before buying the coin. (The magnification readily reveals even the most careful soldering job.)

Adding a mint mark is the most common way to counterfeit a coin. However, it is not the only way. In other cases, counterfeiters have created false dies by taking mirror impressions from real coins. They have then used these dies to strike counterfeit pieces. Attempts such as this, however, usually produce a coin that is not sharply defined and any collector with a good eye can detect one.

Another type of counterfeit is referred to as the privately-made restrike. During the nineteenth century, the U.S. Mint would routinely sell its old dies to scrap metal recyclers. Occasionally, a few of these dies would wind up in private hands and, rather than be melted, as they were supposed to be, would be used to strike coins (coining presses are readily available privately). One example of this is the 1804 "restrike" cent. Discarded dies from an 1803 cent (altered to read 1804) obverse and 1820 reverse were used to strike 1804 coins. However, this unlikely die combination, coupled with the fact that the dies were rusty, resulting in raised bumps all over the surface of the struck coins, makes these coins easily distinguishable from the genuine originals. Other mint-made restrikes exist, but they are not considered counterfeits since they were struck at the government's facility.

Counterfeiters are always working to make money from fake rare coins. With the advent of Teletype services between dealers, modern high-power magnifiers, certification services, and slabs, however, it has become increasingly difficult for them to get their coins into the hands of collectors. (One recent problem has been counterfeit slabbed coins. However, the various certification services have taken steps to correct this problem, such as including holograms, bar codes, security seals, and other covert devices in their plastic holders.)

ALTERED COINS

The term counterfeit could be loosely applied to coins in this category, but generally speaking, an altered coin is a genuine piece whose surfaces have been changed, either chemically or physically, to improve its appearance and, therefore, enhance its monetary value. Remember, the difference between a coin which is graded MS-63 and one which is graded MS-65 can be hundreds, even thousands, of dollars. If an unscrupulous person can remove just a few scratches, bag marks, or other defects on the coin, the improvement can be worth a great deal of money.

The most common way to alter a coin is by "whizzing." Whizzing is a term used in the trade to mean harshly cleaning the coin's surface. It is done by attaching an extremely fine wire brush to a drill and then passing it over the surface.

Whizzed coins have a bright, shiny appearance. They are almost always offered to newcomers who go for the shine of a coin rather than the detail. An experienced collector or a dealer would almost never be fooled by a whizzed coin, because the process itself would remove some of the detail and leave tiny scratches. A whizzed coin has both brilliance and wear—which is impossible on a coin that hasn't been tampered with. A keen eye can often spot this type of fake.

A "processed" coin can be more difficult to detect. In processing, a coin is dipped in a variety of chemical solutions. The solutions are intended to improve the appearance of the piece and get it graded higher.

The methods of processing a coin are varied. They include dipping it in acid washes, baking it in a potato in the oven (used with copper coins to improve appearance), applying abrasive powders and so forth.

While detecting a processed coin can be made difficult, it is not impossible. But it does require the use of a high-powered (10X) magnifier. With the aid of the glass, the dealer or experienced collector will notice such indicators as microscopic pits (the result of the corrosive action of acids), minute hairline scratches (caused by the use of abrasives), or other signs that are inconsistent with the normal surface qualities of a coin. And since collectors prefer, even demand, coins that are in their original, untampered state of preservation, you should shy away from coins that display these characteristics. Resist the temptation to equate bright and shiny with high quality.

An experienced dealer can almost always detect fake coins. If you're paying serious money for rare coins, you should have a dealer who will carefully go over those coins for you. *NOTE: Any reputable dealer will repurchase a coin from you if it turns out to be fake.*

NORMAL COIN DEFECTS

It's important to understand that just because a coin is pitted, scratched, or hairlined doesn't mean that it is counterfeit or altered. Copper and silver coins stored next

U.S. 1904 Liberty head, or Barber type, half dollar.

to paper containing sulphur compounds (a common chemical used in the manufacture of many paper products) are often pitted or discolored. Additionally, coins stored in plastic containers whose make-up is not chemically inert will often react with that plastic causing stains to appear on the coins. The biggest culprit is a plastic called polyvinylchloride (PVC), commonly used for coin holders in the 1960s and 1970s (and still in limited use today). Stay away from PVC, and choose holders that are made of mylar, plexigas, or other inert ingredients. The slight additional cost could translate into additional value, in the future, particularly where long term storage is necessary.

These normal aging processes should not be confused with counterfeit or altered coins. In most cases, they detract from value. But in some cases, where the tarnish, or "toning," on a silver coin takes on multicolored hues of blue, green, gold, or pink, the result can be stunning. The coin will actually increase in "eye appeal," and therefore value, since many collectors look specifically for these coins and prize them highly. Many coins actually acquire a "patina" that make them appear to be little works of art.

CONCLUSION

Coin collecting is a wonderful hobby. It opens up the past as nothing else can. When you hold a coin of Ancient Lydia or Rome in your hands, you can feel the presence of other lives and other worlds. In the process of acquiring the coins, you learn about civilization and history.

And then there is profit. As noted earlier, rare coins have been one of the most profitable, if not the single most profitable, investment vehicle over the past twenty years. Think of it. Not only can you acquire something that reaches out to you with the wisdom and knowledge of the centuries, but also allows you to sell it for a profit in the future!

Finally, there is the matter of beauty. Coins are, indeed, miniature works of art. Some, such as the Gobrecht and Saint-Gaudens designs have been favorably compared with Picassos and Rembrandts. Yet, while you must be wealthy beyond belief to own original works of the masters, for a reasonable price you can afford the great art of coins.

Few people ever regret starting a coin collection—the hobby is rewarding in so many ways. The only people with regrets are those who never began.

COIN RESOURCES

The following periodicals and organizations are good resources for coin collecting:

Periodicals

COINage Magazine
2660 East Main St.
Ventura, CA 93003
  Monthly magazine

Coin Dealer Newsletter
("The Greysheet")
PO Box 11099
Torrance, CA 90510
  Weekly guide to coin prices

Coin World
PO Box 150
Sidney, OH 45367
  Weekly newspaper

Coins Magazine (Monthly)
Numismatic News (Weekly)
c/o Krause Publications
700 E. State St.
Iola, WI 54990

The Numismatist
American Numismatic Association
PO Box 2366
Colorado Springs, CO 80901
  Monthly magazine

Organizations

American Numismatic Association
818 N. Cascade
Colorado Springs, CO 80903

American Numismatic Society (For more advanced collectors)
Broadway and 155th St.
New York, NY 10332

Grading Services

ANACS (American Numismatic Association Certification Services)
818 N. Cascade
Colorado Springs, CO 80903

PCGS (Professional Coin Grading Service—coins are submitted by dealer-members)
PO Box 9458
Newport Beach, CA 92658

NGC (Numismatic Guaranty Corporation)
PO 1776
Parsippany, NJ 07054

INDEX